THE RAJNITI

THE RAJNITI;

OR

TALES,

EXHIBITING

THE MORAL DOCTRINES AND THE CIVIL AND MILITARY POLICY OF THE HINDOOS

LALLU LAL AND J.R. A. S. LOWE

GYAN

Published by

Gyan Publishing House
5, Ansari Road
Daryaganj, New Delhi-110002
Phone: 011-47034999, 9811692060
E-mail: books@gyanbooks.com

Distribution Network
gyanbooks.com
India, USA, Canada, UK, Australia

ISBN: 978-93-6920-326-0 (PB)

First Published, 1809

2nd Impression 2025

Printed at: Gyan Press, Delhi.

THE RAJNITI
Author: LALLU LAL AND J.R. A. S. LOWE

RAJNÍTÍ;

OR,

TALES,

EXHIBITING

THE MORAL DOCTRINES AND THE CIVIL AND MILITARY POLICY OF THE HINDOOS.

TRANSLATED LITERALLY FROM THE HINDI OF SHRÍ LALLÚ LAL KAB, INTO ENGLISH,

BY ENSIGN J. R. A. S. LOWE,

INTERPRETER AND QR. MR. 11TH REGIMENT N. I.

CALCUTTA:

PRINTED AND PUBLISHED BY P. S. D'ROZARIO AND CO., TANK-SQUARE.

1853.

PREFACE.

In order to facilitate the study of Hindi, at all times attended with difficulties, and under the impression that an English version of the RAJNITI may afford the desired assistance to Military Officers studying for the reward lately sanctioned by Government, the Translator has been induced to publish this book, trusting that all errors therein contained may be viewed with indulgence, as it has no kind of pretension to any merit beyond that of being a Literal Translation of the Original Hindi Work.

J. R. A. S. LOWE, ENSIGN,

Inter. and Qr. Mr. 11*th Regt. N. I.*

Allahabad, 16*th May* 1853.

RAJNÍTÍ.

O elephant-faced bestower of ease, dispeller of the world's grief,
O Gunesh, fulfil my desires, O son of Sumbhoo, chief of the world!

At a certain time Shrí Narain Pundit made a collection of stories from Moral Philosophy into Sanskrit. Having made one book he called its name Hitopadesa. Then in the year 1869 Shri Lallújí Lal Kab, a Guzarati Brahmin, of the Sahasr Awdich family, resident of Agra, extracting the essential meaning thereof, and putting it into the Brij Language, gave (the book) the name of Rajniti.

COUPLET.

Those who are learned and wise understand the subject of the narrative,
But the ignorant think within themselves what is this that Lal has written.
The Language of Brij, says every one, is like unto the voice of the Deity,
All Poets extol it, deeming it the origin of infinite taste.

By reading and hearing this Rajniti, people become proficient in the Brij dialect, and every thing relating to the customs of the world in them they become accomplished.

First in that book it is thus written, "That those who are learned, they regarding themselves as indecayable and immortal, fix their thoughts on science and wealth, and that when any one reflects that their tuft of hair is seized by death, they then practice virtue." Again it is thus said, "That among all rarities, the rarity of the figure Knowledge is principal, because the provider of food, the guide to the road of virtue, and ever the bestower of wisdom it is; in which no sharer can take a part, and it has no price, it is not decayable. This is a hidden treasure, this thieves, thugs (kind of thief) nor kings can take away by practising stratagem. Knowledge produces mildness; having acquired mildness, one becomes worthy; having become worthy, wealth is acquired; having got wealth, one practises virtue; from virtue one remains happy: as a river is conducted by a canal to the Sea, so indeed does knowledge take a man unto the King, after that, as it is written in his destiny so does he reap the fruit thereof. The science of arms and the science of religious books, these two in the world are the bestowers of high rank, but in old age, people beholding the science of arms, ridicule it, and from the science of books is more celebrity acquired. Therefore from infancy it is incumbent on man to make a compilation of books; because where a learned man has access, there a wealthy man cannot go. Therefore, under pretence of telling stories, I instruct children in political science, because at first children's minds do not fix on religious books. Again, it is even so said: Whoever in childhood you teach science, he never forgets it: as in a fresh earthern vessel whatever you put, its quality it absorbs. From this then having fashioned five different kinds of stories, I now relate them. The first: The Acquisition of Friends; that is, the mode of forming friendship. The second: Breach of Friendship; that is, the method of estranging the affections. The third: War; that is, the manner of conducting a battle. The fourth: Peace; that is, the art of forming a negotiation, and the fifth: Loss of Possession; that is, having obtained any thing to throw it away.

BOOK THE FIRST.

Acquisition of Friends.

Here is the Story's commencement.

Although to a poet residing in a well-house a narrative is a boundless ocean, yet I relate somewhat just as my dull understanding enables me:

On the banks of the Shri Gunga (Holy Ganges) is a town by name Patna, there the abode of all skill, the very wise, virtuous king by name Sudursun resided. He one day learned from some Pundit a distich, of which the meaning is this:

"Various kinds of doubts it dissipates and makes manifest the meaning of abstruse phrases, therefore learning is the eye of every one. He who has not the eye of the figure learning, he is blind. And youth, wealth, supremacy, inconsiderate actions, these four, each of them, is the cause of danger, and where these four are, there how know you what may be."

Having heard this, the King, seeing the ignorance of his sons, having reflected, began to say,—"That for such a son to be born of what use is it?" He who is without having acquired learning and void of virtue such a son is as a blind eye which is not to see with, but if it come to smart, then it causes pain. It is said "Call him a son by whose birth his family's increase (of rank) is obtained, else of a truth then in the world is not he born to die? But correct and learned whatever son may be born in a family that man is the lion of it. Just as the heavens derive splendour from the moon, so does a family from that son. He whose name among the number of the learned has not been written by the pen, his mother is called barren, and for their alms-giving, devotion, bravery, learning and earning wealth, those who have acquired no renown, their mothers have only by bringing them forth suffered distress; but have seen no comfort in their sons." They say,—"That those who in great pilgrimages have undergone very severe penance and fasting, their sons are obedient, wealthy, learned and virtuous." These six things are the givers of happiness in the world:—the continual acquisition of wealth; a body free from disease; love from the wife; a wife sweet spoken; an obedient son, and learning producing riches. Having said thus much, again the King observed, Oh that my son were talented, it would indeed be well. Hearing this, some one in the royal assembly said, O great King! Life, action, wealth, knowledge and death, these five things were formed from the womb for every one having a body; therefore what is in destiny that without taking place remaineth not: just as the nakedness of the holy Mahádéva and the bed of serpents of (Vishnu) Bhugwan. For this reason then be not thoughtful; if in the destiny of your sons, knowledge be written, then will they be learned.

Again the King replied: This indeed is true, but to man the Almighty has given hands and understanding, this was for the purpose of learning knowledge. As with one wheel a chariot does not run, so without the exertions of man work is not accomplished. Therefore strive always and sit not still trusting to fate. It is said, "That just as a potter having taken clay, whatever he wishes to make of it that he makes, so also man reaps the reward according to his actions. Fate (1) is inert: of it nothing can come. Endeavour is the doer, therefore if the doer stimulate Fortune, then good or evil happen from the combination of Endeavour and Fortune. But to remain only trusting to Fate, is the act of a degenerate being, and that mother and father of a son who do not force learning upon him, them regard as hostile." It is said, "That an ignorant son shines not in the society of the learned, as among ducks, a heron does not appear well."

After this the King thinking thus, having made an assembly of Pundits,

(1) For this passage I am indebted to Professor Hall, Benares College.

said, O Pundits! is there any among you so learned, who can give to my sons a new life by counselling them to walk in the path of virtue? It is said "as glass by keeping company with gold appears like the emerald, thus by the society of good men acquiring knowledge, a blockhead becomes learned, and by society with men of low habits he becomes low."

COUPLET.

Associate with good men, for they dispel the pains of others,
But in the fruitless society of the base, every hour there is violence.

These having heard the words of the King, Vishnu Surma, an aged Brahmin, acquainted with all Moral Philosophy like Brihaspati (Jupiter), spoke: O great King! the Princes are worthy of being educated, but do not impart knowledge to the unworthy: because were he to read, it would not be successful, and if it were profitable, then he would commit infinite injustice; abandoning the virtues of learning, he would stedfastly bind the knot of vice. Therefore instruct not the degenerate. As feed a cat with fresh and fresh food (daily) yet it would not forsake its feline propensities. Again, bestow a hundred efforts and teach the heron yet it will not talk like the parrot: and though it be perfect in the theory of religion yet it will only learn still better how to lay wait to kill fish. O great King! in your family no offspring without virtuous principles can be born: as in a mine of rubies glass would not be generated. We sell not knowledge. I take nothing from you, but it is your desire: therefore in six months very easily I will make your sons perfect in the road of morality.

Having heard this, the King said to the aged Brahmin Vishnu Surma, Ah! by association with the flower, behold small insects truly ascend the foreheads of excellent persons, therefore by your company what cannot take place? Just as when a stone is consecrated, all men regarding it as a deity, worship it. As on the mountain Udeachal (1) at the rising of the sun, all things appear like unto the sun, so by good company an ignoble man attains celebrity.

METRE OF FOUR LINES.

The large bee so keeps the insect under its breast
That it changes the insect's form like its own constantly.
Iron becomes gold by a touch of the Philosopher's stone,
This in this world I have frequently seen.

(1) *Udeachal* is the Eastern Mountain, behind which the Sun is supposed to rise.

COUPLET.

Sesh,(1) Saridá, Byas Muni, can find no way of expressing it,
The praises of good society, how then can an ignorant man tell forth.

You are capable of making my sons learned. Thus did that King with humility deliver over his sons to the Brahmin. Then that Brahmin taking the King's sons with him went and sat in a lofty palace. Finding an opportunity he said: Hearken, O sons of the great King!

COUPLET.

The time of the sensible passes with pleasure in poetical writings,
But the days of the ignorant in slumber and dissipation.

I now relate the story "Acquisition of Friends," because in the acquisition of friends is a great advantage.

For one Chitragriva (painted neck) a pigeon and a tortoise, an antelope and a rat were great friends. Of their meeting and their actions I will now tell you. That those who are weak and without wealth but between whom and the wise there is friendship, their work is accomplished just as was that of the crow, tortoise, antelope and rat. Having heard this the Princes said, What is that story? Then Vishnu Surma relates it:

On the banks of the river Godáveri is a Semul (or cotton) tree, on which birds coming from all quarters roosted. One day at dawn, Lughupatnak by name, a crow, awoke up. He beholding at a distance a death-visaged fowler approaching him, began to caw, and said, To-day at time of dawn I have seen an impious vicious face,(2) there is no knowing then what will happen. Thus reflecting Lughupatnak the crow flew away. It is said, "That in places of violence the learned remain not sagacious and fools by sitting therein endure fear and sorrow." In the mean while the fowler having cast some grains of rice under a tree, spread his net over them. Thither, Chitragriva, the pigeon, together with his family, happened to come. Among them one bird seeing the pieces of rice, said, I wish to pick them up. Chitragriva said, Ho! In this wood from whence hath rice come? this is some trick. Therefore these do not appear good unto me.

(1.) *Sesh:*—The King of the serpent race, of a thousand heads, forming both couch and canopy of Vishnu, and also upholder of the world, which rests on one of its heads. *Saridá:*—A name of Saraswati, wife of Brahma, goddess of speech and eloquence, and patroness of music and the arts, and inventress of the Sanskrit Language into the Devanagri character. *Byas:*—A celebrated saint and author, supposed to be the original compiler of the Vedas and Puranas, and founder of the Vedanta Philosophy.

(2.) A fear that Hindus entertain on seeing an evil omen early in the day.

If you covet after these grains of rice it will so happen as when, through coveting a bracelet, the traveller fell into a quagmire and became the food of an aged tiger. Having heard this the birds enquired, What is that story like? Then Chitragriva, the prince of pigeons, said:

One day I was in a forest; there I saw that an old tiger having bathed in the water and with kush (1) in his hand had come and seated himself in the road. Meanwhile a traveller, a Brahmin, came that way. He when he perceived the tiger seated, then being frightened, on that very spot stood amazed. Seeing him terrified, the tiger said, Hola! Deity. I who am seated in the road, it is for the purpose of performing a virtuous action, and in my possession is a golden bracelet, I give it you for the Divine Krishn's sake, you take it. Hearing this he thought within himself, To-day it appears as if my fortune had awoke; but to enter into such doubts is not expedient, because, if you receive from the bad, good things, afterwards it causes distress. If in the water of life there be poison, then indeed must it be fatal, again it is so said: That without exertion wealth is not obtained, and where exertion is made there reward is reaped. Just as where there is treasure there is a snake; where a flower there a thorn; (in fine) without undergoing pain no comfort. Having thus reflected, the Brahmin said to him: where is that bracelet? He stretching out his hand showed it. Then the Brahmin was seized with avarice and said: you are a worker of evil, how can I place confidence in you? The tiger replied, Ho! For one thing having bathed at dawn of day and become generous I am seated; secondly, I have become old; therefore I have lost my claws, teeth and power of the organs of sense, now wherefore will you not place confidence in me? It is said, Sacrifice, reading the Vedas, almsgiving, devotion, virtue, patience, forgiveness, contentedness, these eight kinds they say are not to be found in hypocrites. I of my own free will wish to give it you; other tigers eat flesh, that is not my case. But those who do not know it speak thus of me. Just as if a bawd should admonish persons to be virtuous, then indeed people would not believe her, and should a Brahmin be a murderer yet would he be revered; therefore you are right. My body has become old and with this body have I comitted much sin. Thus reflecting, having cast aside all sin I have read in religious books and heard, It is expedient for a living being that as a man's life is dear to him, so he con-

(1) *Kush*:—The sacred grass of Hindos (Poa cynosuroides).

sider every one, and four kinds of charity are bestowed; one for the sake of religion, another for fear, a third for the assistance of others and the fourth for love's sake—this is not so with me, I merely considering you in distressed circumstances, give to you. Shri Krishn Chand did truly say unto King Udhistur: Give alms to the poor, then will your reward be the greater. Because medicine and medicinal diet are given to those in pain not to those enjoying ease, and if on perceiving that both the country and the time are worthy any bestow their alms, those alms call ye beneficial, therefore O Brahmin! wash you in the tank and return: being pure receive the gift. Listening unto his words, being overcome with avarice, even as he descended into the tank so did he stick fast in the mire. When he could not extract his feet from the mire, then the tiger moved quietly towards him. The Brahmin said, oh! why are you coming? The tiger replied, tarry you awhile in the water, I having caused the Priog(1) to be read over you and given the bracelet, will listen to the sound of the Swast.(2) Repeating this, having gone near to him, and seeing him stuck fast, he seized him by the throat. Then the Brahmin began to say in his own mind, "nothing avails by teaching the wicked religious books and the Vedas; because no one forsakes his natural bent. Just as the milk of a cow is by nature sweet and has nought to do with what it eats and drinks; and he whose passions are not in subjection, his acts are just like the bathing of an elephant, how much soever you wash it, again it becomes the same as ever. Therefore I have not done well in that I have placed confidence in the tiger. Every one follows the customs of his race." Whilst he was thus reflecting, the tiger having slain him, made him his food, therefore I say, that you should never perform any act without deliberation.

VERSE OF FOUR LINES.

Without reflection he who performs an act afterwards repents.
He who destroys his own work becomes a ridicule in this world;
In the world he becomes a ridicule; in his mind he obtains no ease;
Eating, drinking, esteem, pleasure come not even within his thoughts.

Girdhur, (3) the chief of poets, has said: Grief is in no way removed by the mere casting it aside, it pierces the heart of him who acts without thought. It is said: "Digested food, a learned son, a chaste wife, a well served King, and to speak and act with thought from these, no harm will

(1) *Priog*:—A kind of prayer used by a Hindu on the occasion of his offering a gift.

(2) *Swast*:—A benediction, Amen, Be it so तथास्तु Be it so, yes.

(3) *Girdhur*, a famous poet.

ever arise." Having heard this, one bird cried out: Ho! how long shall we think over in adversity this old one's words? Entertain such doubts then how shall we manage for food! For in food and water there is doubt. If thus we continue thinking then indeed will our lives not pass in comfort. It is said, that the avaricious, impatient, irritable, ever-suspecting, he who entertains a desire for another's fortune, the exceeding merciful; these six ever remain distressed. Having said thus much that bird descended to pick up the rice, along with him all descended. Then Chitragriva reflected: that with them happen what will, yet it is not right to leave their company. It is said "Although a man having read many religious books may have given advice to others, yet when avarice comes and surrounds him then his knowledge availeth him not."

Then along with them Chitragriva also descended, and when those birds came into the net, then at whose bidding they had descended, him, they began to censure. Thus it is elsewhere said, "That in an assembly coming forward should any perform an act which shall turn out well, then all reap an equal reward, but if mismanaged, then they would censure him who had come forward."

Hearing their reproach Chitragriva said: Oh! It is no fault of this one. When misfortune comes then even a friend becomes inimical: just as the thigh of the cow becomes a pillar to tie the calf to.

COUPLET.

The sportsman wounded a deer with an arrow, but its blood pointed it out. Intimate friends become unfriendly, O Toolsie, in hard times.

Though a man may have studied Astrology and Scripture, and know even all anent the three times (present, past, and future) yet when that which is predestined comes to pass then his divine knowledge is upset.

therefore he is a friend who in adversity becomes of service, and to grieve for that which is past is the act of a fool. Therefore be patient, contrive some means of escape. It is said:

STANZA.

What is past, let that be forgotten, take thought for the future;
That which can be easily accomplished, to that give your attention;
To that give your mind which can be performed;
That neither the wicked may ridicule you or you experience distress of mind.
The chief of poets, Girdhur, has said: rely on this in your mind,
That for the future there is consolation by regarding the past as past.

Again it is said, "That fortitude in adversity; humility in prosperity; in assemblies eloquence in speech: bravery in war; desire after renown;

thirst for reading; these are the habits of great men. And man must ever abandon six faults: sleep, impatience, fear, anger, laziness, grief."

Having said thus much, again Chitragrava said, Now being all unanimous exert your strength, lift up the net and fly away with it. Thus it is said, "If a few joining together act as one, then great works are performed; as having joined grass together they twist a cord, so with it an elephant is tied fast."

Hearing this, all exerting their strength, took the net and flew off, and when the fowler saw that they had gone far away, then said he in his own mind: Now truly all are of one mind, they will descend, then well I look to them. When the net did not descend on the earth, then the fowler sat down, being in despair. Thither the birds began to say to Chitragriva, Oh King! the fowler remains truly, having given up all hope of our flesh; but how shall we now get free from the net? Chitragriva replied: Oh hearken! In this world a mother, a father and a friend, these three even by nature show affection. Therefore a friend of mine by name Hiranyak, a rat, dwells in the Bichitr wood on the banks of the river Gunduki, thither let us proceed, then he will cut our cords asunder. Thus considering they went to the door of the rat, and there was seated at his door verily Hiranyak. He seeing the birds coming, entering his hole remained silent. Then Chitragriva said, friend come out. Recognizing his friend's voice, having come forth, he said: to-day how great is my fortune in that my friend Chitragriva, showing fävor on me, has come to pay me a visit. And seeing the birds in the net, he said: My friend what is this? He replied: friend, this is the sin of their former birth. In one's destiny as it is written so reapeth that one the reward thereof, and disease, grief, bonds, and pains are the fruits of one's own acts committed. It is said:—

VERSE.

Should the Sun rise shining in the west corner, there would be no harm therein, or should the lotus blossom on the mountain and Sumeroo move then let it move sometimes.

Fire also at times becomes cold, but thus reflecting hath Moteeram said, The lines written by fate cannot be effaced, this even is held correct in the Vedas(1) and Puranas.(2)

(1) *Vedas.*—The Indian Scripture, believed by the Hindus to have been revealed by Brahma, and preserved by tradition till compiled, arranged and divided into four parts: Rig, Yajush, Sama and Atharva, by a sage styled Vyasa.

(2) *Purana.*—A sacred and poetical work, supposed to have been compiled or composed by the poet Vyasa. There are eighteen Puranas, which comprise the whole body of Hindu Theology.

Having heard this, the rat began to gnaw the threads that fastened Chitragriva. Then Chitragriva, king of pigeons, said, Oh friend, first cut the bonds of my comrades, then afterwards cut mine. The rat replied: friend, these cords are hard and my teeth are tender: therefore first I will cut your fastening, then after that if I can cut them, I will cut those of the others. Chitragriva said: This is not the act of a chieftain; to leave his comrades bound and himself escape. For this reason if these get their release first, then can my release be accomplished. Then the rat said: Brother! It is not customary for one to leave off talking of oneself and to speak of others. It is said, "that having suffered distress, preserve wealth, giving up wealth protect your wife, and when wealth and wife both go, then let them go, but preserve yourself; because virtue, wealth, action, and liberation, these four blessings are retained by preserving life, and by its departure they go with it. Again Chitragriva said, Friend! Such indeed is morlity, but being learned, it is expedient to show mercy to refugees. It is said, "give both wealth and life for the sake of others, because one day assuredly the body will be destroyed." Therefore if it be of use for the sake of others what can be better? For this reason abandon all plans for preserving my perishable body, and an immortal and imperishable renown, that contrive to preserve for me. It is said "Everlasting renown is obtained from the perishable body, and from the unclean things clean:" therefore between the body and fame there is a great difference. Having heard this, Hiranyak being delighted, said, my friend, owing to your affection for these your dependants, know that the sovereignty of the three worlds is yours. Saying this he gnawed the fastenings of them all and said: friends, through the fault of your understanding were you ensnared, now grieve not in your minds. It is said, "that birds can discern at a distance of eight miles grain which lies scattered on the ground, but they see not the net." Therefore there is no blame to your understanding, because even the Moon and the Sun suffer the pain of an eclipse, and both elephants and snakes fall into snares; the learned become indigent, and at one time beasts, birds, aërial and aquatic, being in the power of another, suffer distress, what is predestined without taking place remaineth not.

Thus Hiranyak having instructed, and having caused him to listen to pleasing conversation, entertained Chitragriva together with all his retinue and dismissed them; and he himself retired into his hole. Then Lughuputnak, the crow, who on seeing the fowler flew away, he having heard these news said in his own mind, that in the world friendship is a great rarity. See in what a situation a friend is of service. Thus reflecting, flying off the tree and going to the door of the rat, he said, Oh Hiranyak, my respects to you, and knowing you to be a great person, I have come to form friendship with you. Having heard this (address), Hiranyak said, Hola! who art thou? He replied: I am a crow, by name Lughuputnak. Hearing this, Hiranyak laughing, said: what kind of freidship can there be between me and thee? and to form friendship with an enemy is the root of distress, and I am your food, you my devourer, therefore where you think there is friendshig there make it. Among heterogeneous animals there is no amity, should there be, it would be just as when a deer was ensnared through a jackal, and a crow caused its liberation. The crow said, what kind of story is that? Then the rat relates it:

In the Magadh (1) country there is a forest by name Champak(2). There for sometime on a Champa (3) tree dwelt a crow, named Suboodh, and below it an antelope, named Chitragud: between those two there was a great intimacy. Then one day a certain jackal observing the antelope to be fat and plump, reflected in his own mind: If I form friendship with this one then shall I get this one's flesh to eat. Thus meditating coming unto the antelope he said: My friend, yon are in excellent health. The antelope said, Friend who art thou? Then said he to the antelope, my name is Chudrbudh, a jackal, in this forest without having made a friend, friendless alone I live. To-day have I obtained a sight of you, I am comforted now, I will remain beneath your feet. Having thus formed his conversation, he joined himself to him. At evening then the antelope set out for his own abode and he also accompained him. At length proceeding on and on, having come thither where the antelope's friend the crow was, the crow seeing the jackal said: my friend, this second one with you who is he? The antelope replied, This is Chudrbudh by name, a jackal, who is desirous of forming friendship with me. The crow said, my friend form no intimacy quickly with one of another country and unknown to you. It is said, He whose nature, disposition, abode you do not know, with him form not friendship, and this is morality that you do not even lodge such an one in your house, for you know not how it may turn out.

(1) *Magadh* is the name of the country, including Patna, Gya, &c.

(2) *Champak.*—A forest of Gold.

(3) *Champa.*— A gold colored flower tree (Michelia champaca.)

Just as unwittingly granting a lodging to a male cat, the poor bird, the vulture, was slain. The antelope asked, What is that story? Then the crow relates:

On the banks of the Ganges is a mountain called Girdhurkoot (1) where stood a certain citron-leaved Indian fig tree, in the hollow of which dwelt a very old vulture. There other birds brought their food, out of it they gave him a little also, by which he existed, and when the birds used to go to pick up food, then the vulture used to act as guardian to their little ones.

One day a male cat, by name Derugh Hurun (long eared), climbed up the tree for the purpose of devouring the bird's little ones. On seeing him the little birds cried out: then the vulture hearing their cry, putting his head out of the hollow said, Ho! who is this? Then the male cat seeing the vulture, being alarmed, began to say within his own mind, If I shall fly from hence, this one rushing after me will kill me; therefore by going up to him will matters turn out right. Thus having reflected, assuming a mild disposition, going near unto the vulture, having made his obeisance, he said, you are great. The vulture said, who art thou and hither wherefore hast thou come? Keep at a distance, else even now will I slay thee. The male cat replied, master, first hear the reason of my coming, then afterwards whatever is to your heart's wish that you can do. I have preserved the Brahmachay (2) (penance), and I have made a vow to keep the Chandrayan fast,(3) just now as I was coming from bathing in the Holy Ganges in the road I heard of your renown from the mouth of birds, that you are perfect in your discourses on knowledge of a religious kind, therefore I have come to listen to your religious counsels, and my conviction is this; that if I remain some days in the society of such a virtuous one, I shall then become pure. It is said:—

COUPLET.

Much discretion effaceth wickedness from the heart;
O Lal, the society of the good dispels much wickedness.

(1) *Girdhurkut.*—Vulture fort, a mountain close to Goburdhun.

(2) *Brahmachay* is the profession and way of living of a religious student or Brahmin, from the time he is invested with the sacerdotal thread till he has finished his studies and become a householder or girhist, or for a period of 12 years, during which time he cooks and does every thing for himself, besides only eating once, and that at even time.

(3) *Chandrayan* Fast, means, that a Hindu, as the moon increases or decreases, so he also increases or diminishes his food the weight of one rupee or a tola, and on seeing the moon every day, after performing his adorations to it, he partakes of some food, having fasted all the previous part of the day.

This indeed is my desire—notwithstanding this, if you wish to kill me, then slay me. It is said: "That a householder should show respect even towards an enemy when he comes into his house, as the tree when one comes to cut it down casts its shade over him. Therefore if even a child come to the house of an old man as a guest, then is he worthy of being served (at such times) there is no thought given to age. If a guest come to the house, regard him superior to all, as is right, so show him respect, and if there be nothing else in the house, then give him sweet words, a grass bedding and cold water, and with great affection sit together; and if even so much be not done, then from whosoever's house a guest goes away despairing (of reception), he bears away all his virtues and gives unto him his own sins. Therefore the good take compassion on the ignorant, as the moon disperses her light on every place." The vulture answered: Male cats have an excessive liking to flesh, and here the young of birds dwell, therefore to you I am unable to say anything. If you remain here, then act not treacherously with these little ones.

Hearing this, the male cat, touching the ground with his paws, stroking his ears,(1) said, Master, from me such indeed will never come. Having heard and read the Dharmshastr, or religious books, I have taken on me the state of a hermit, and it is great impiety to kill life. In all religious books it is forbidden. It is said, a good man must be such that he bear with another's sins, protect all, then will he attain unto heaven. There is no doubt in this, because virtue is ever an assistant, and he whose flesh you eat he indeed departeth this life; to the eater for one moment only the taste thereof remaineth on the tongue, therefore as your own, so regard every one's life. It is said, "If with bulbs, roots, fruit, flowers, and leaves the belly can be filled, then wherefore kill life?"

Thus saying, having increased the other's confidence in him, the male cat remained near the vulture. Finding an opportunity, he took and seized two or four of the birds' young ones. When those young ones cried out, then the vulture would say, Oh Derughkurun, wherefore have you brought away these little ones? He would reply, master, my children are separated from me; for their sakes I pass away the day with these.

Having thus said, when he had fulfilled his desire, then the male cat fled from thence, and the birds coming and finding the bones and skins of

(1) A Hindu mode of procedure, often accompanied by an exclamation such as Ram! Ram!—the motion of the hands meaning to express, Be that far from me.

their little ones lying near the hollow of the vulture, then thought they that our little ones this sinful treacherous one and of low caste has devoured. Thus thinking, all joining together, they beat the life out of the vulture. Therefore I say that unwittingly form not friendship.

Hearing these words, the jackal, being enraged, said, my friend, on the day that you formed friendship with the antelope, that day this one what did he know about your race and disposition that he sat together with you? Therefore to say this is a relation or a stranger is the act of the foolish; to the learned all are as his relations. As the antelope is my friend, so also are you, and the good or evil in one is ascertained by his habits. The antelope said: my friends, wherefore make you this altercation; as long as you remain in harmony together so much the better. The crow said, Brother, you know. In the mean time they all went, each one thinking about his food, and returning in the evening met together. In this way they began to remain there.

Some days after the jackal, finding the antelope alone, said: my friend, I have come from seeing a good green field of tender barley for you, if you walk my way then will I show it you. In this manner, acting with subterfuge, he led him astray, and he, overcome with desire, being avaricious, rushed up and went in company with him. Thus every day going with him, and having eaten, would he return.

One day, the man keeping watch over that field, seeing that antelope coming, laid a snare. The instant he entered to graze, he was immediately entrapped. Then began he to say in his mind, that, beside a friend who will extricate me from this difficulty? And on the other hand, the jackal, seeing him snared, dancing about, began to say in his mind: The fruit of my deceit I shall this day reap. When the watchman shall have eaten his flesh, then whatever flesh remains attached to the bones and skin, that will I eat. This one truly at this idea remained dancing about, and the antelope thought: this one, seeing my distress, being perplexed, is beating his hands and feet, but he knew not this, that one, avaricious of a gift, tumbles about like a juggler. Then, seeing the state of the jackal, the antelope said, Brother, for my sake wherefore do you manifest such sorrow? It is said, "one who is of service in adversity, he is a friend; he who dies in the battle, is a hero; in poverty prove a wife: in distress prove a friend.—Thus said the antelope. Then the jackal going near, perceived: That this one is fallen into a severe snare, thereby my heart's desire will readily be fulfilled. Thus reflecting, he said, Brother! this net is made of catgut, and mine is the fast of the Sun, how shall I seize it with my teeth and cut it? If it had been any other fast, then would there not have been a thought on the matter; but in the fast of the Sun day there is this to be thought of: if it be broken, then all former penance would become fruitless. Therefore to-day it is so, to-morrow morning whatever can be accomplished by me that will I perform. Thus saying, having retreated, he sat down.

In the mean time the night became past and there Suboodh by name, the crow, awoke up. He cawing began to say: That during the night my friend returned not, now will I search for him somewhere. Saying this, he set out from thence. Proceeding on, he saw indeed that he was fast in a snare. The crow said, Friend, what is this? He replied, Friend I heeded not your saying,—this is the fruit of it. Again said the crow, That new friend of your's, where is he? He replied: That one, coveting my flesh, will be even here. Then said the crow, Brother, a good man considers every one's disposition like unto his own, and this is a wicked man's natural disposition, that who ever acts well towards him he does him harm. It is said, "A wicked person coming without being called first, falls at your feet, afterwards, whispering in your ear, by way of affection, he shows friendship; acting with deceit he points out an evil way, and finding an opportunity he takes advantage of it. Just as the Gnat coming behind the back, attaching itself to the ear, watching its opportunity, stings you, so a wicked man is even like it. Therefore I say, never place confidence in an enemy. It is also said:

STANZA.

An enemy, a captive, a shop-keeper, a gamester, a thief, a liar,
An adulterer, a diseased man, a debtor, a gallant of a town woman,
A gallant of a town woman unwittingly do not trust,
If they each swear hundred upon hundred oaths, give not heed to one of them,
Says Girdhur, chief of poets, he who comes to the house uncalled,
Concocting affectionate speeches, him regard as a perfect enemy.

Having heard these many words, the antelope, taking a long drawn sigh, said: Those who by speaking falsehoods do evil unto others, the burden of them how doth the earth bear? Thus remained they conversing together. In the mean time, seeing the watchman coming, then the crow said to the antelope, Now you, turning up your eyes, remain as dead; when I shall call out, then rise and flee.

Hearing this he did just so. The watchman coming and seeing the antelope, said: this one lieth, having died of himself how can I slay him? Then thinking him to be dead, having opened the fastening, he was about to raise him, when immediately the crow cawed, and the antelope sprung up and ran off. Then the watchman, being vexed, hurled clubs which struck the jackal in the mouth, and on hitting him he died instanter. Thus in another place is it even so written, that: in three days, three nights, three fortnights, three months, three years, the fruit of virtue and vice is constantly reaped.

Having heard this much of the story, Lughuputnak, the crow, said to the rat, Hiranyak: My friend, if perchance I were to devour you, then even would not my belly be filled. Therefore why should I commit evil against one such a friend, so virtuous and good as you: because Chitragriva together with all the birds when they fell into the net, then you, rendering assistance, saved their lives. It is said, "That in order to accomplish your undertaking, you should form friendship with the virtuous, then one day it will come of use." Therefore I wish to seek shelter from you that sometimes in my distress you may render assistance. For this reason have I come, do not you think otherwise. Then said the rat, One should never form friendship with the fickle:

COUPLET.

A crow, a buffalo, a bad man, a wolf and a cat,
All these five by being trusted gain their own advantage.

Therefore in all these never place any confidence. If an enemy remain on terms in his friendship be not mistaken. It is said "Howsoever hot water may be, yet it would not keep from quenching the fire; the weak would not be strong; discordant words would never be agreable. Just as on the water a cart goes not, nor on land a boat." Again it is also said "That you should not tell secret words to your wife; if you do tell her, then do not quarrel with her, if you make war then entertain no hope of your life." Some say even so:

STANZA.

O sire these never displease: a poet, a learned man, a spiritual guide, a friend,
A son, a wife, a door-keeper, one who performs a sacrifice (priest),
A priest, a state minister whoever he may be,
A Brahmin, a neighbour, a physician, and he who cooks for you.
Says Girdhur, prince of Poets, what kind of opinion is this you hold?
That, oh Sire! forsaking these thirteen your work can be performed.

Again the crow said, My friend, what you have said all that have I heard: but this is not my intention that I should do you injury, and if you will not form friendship with me, then, at your door continuing fasting I will give up my life; I swear by Ram and Luchmun. Because the friendship of the bad is destroyed in a few days, even just as an earthern vessel breaking cannot be put together again, and the friendship of the virtuous is such as like a vessel of gold, which breaks not quickly, and if it breaks, then even it can be put in order again, and how many virtuous men are like cocoa-nuts that indeed outside they are hard and within soft? Again the bad verily appear like unto the Ber(1) which above is soft and hard within. Therefore the good and the bad are known by their dispositions: it has nothing to do with their appearance; and the good are pure, generous, brave, modest, affectionate, void of avarice, truth-spoken; the bad would never be so. From this then tell me where one meets with a virtuous person who would not form friendship with him?

Having listened to this form of conversation, the rat Hiranyak, having come out of his hole, said: Having heard your words I have experienced great comfort. Just as one stricken by a hot wind, by bathing and rubbing on sandal over all his limbs becomes cool, so has my heart been refreshed. It is said, "In six ways does friendship become increased—receiving, giving, speaking truths, hearing them, eating, feeding. And these are defects in friendship: to beg ever, to speak unfriendly words, to tell lies, fickleness and gaming: of these however not one even is in you. For this reason, perceiving your good judgment, I am delighted; from to-day you are my friend. Having spoken these many words and having seated the crow at his door, the rat went into his hole, and from thence having brought some articles of food he feasted him and himself sat near unto him. Thus did those two begin to live together.

One day the crow said: Friend rat, at this place food is gathered with very great difficulty, therefore let us proceed thither where you may pick up plenty and with comfort procure somewhat to eat. Then said the rat: My friend it is said "That he who is wise he having put down his front foot raises his hind foot." Therefore first think of a place, then afterwards set out from hence. The crow replied; My friend, I have thought of a good spot. That in Dundkarunye there is a pool, by name

(1) *Ber*:—also called Konar, is the *Zisiphus Jujuba,* the fruit of which ripens in February and is good in allaying thirst, and is also a cure for the राजरोग or consumption.

Kuphoor; there is my friend the tortoise, by name Munthurk, he is wise and virtuous. It is said, "All are learned in giving religious counsel to others, but they who keep themselves stedfast in faith's road they are scarce people." Therefore my friend he putting us up in a suitable manner, will keep us. It is said, "Dreary is that country in which there is no honor to oneself, no acquiring friends or knowledge, nor good society, nor discernment of merit, nor even a place of pilgrimage, then to dwell there is not advisable." The rat said: My friend, thither take me along with you.

Thus conversing together they both went unto the tortoise. Seeing them the tortoise said: My friend Lughuputnuk has come. Saying thus much, advancing, showing him civility, washing his feet with respect and seating him on the carpet, he began to reverence him. Then said the crow, My friend, reverence this one more especially: this one is very virtuous, by name Hiranyak, a rat, the prince of all rats. My mouth is not formed to extol his virtues; if with its thousand mouths Seshnag were to speak then might he describe them. Saying thus much he related the whole ancedote regarding Chitragriva. Then Munthurk, having paid his respects to him, inquired of him: Your residence where is it and how happened it you came here?

Then began the rat to relate: In the town of Champa is a Pagan temple of religious mendicants. In it there dwelt a holy mendicant, by name Churakurun. By asking alms whatever grain he brought he would place it on a high shelf. This grain I used to jump up and devour. Some days after his friend, a holy mendicant, by name Benakurun, came thither. Churakurun talked with him and kept striking the ground with a stick, Then Benakurun said: In that you do not with fitting attention listen unto my words, where then are your thoughts? Then he replied: Oh schoolfellow (*lit.* taught by the same teacher) I am indeed listening to your words with all my heart, but this wretched rat devours all my charity-acquired grain, and gives me great trouble: he is affected with avarice. Brother, contrive a remedy for this. Benakurun said, There is some cause for this. Just as a young woman embracing and kissing an old husband, concealed her paramour, so indeed this rat, without a cause does not jump up. Churakurun said: What is that anecdote? Then Benakuran began to relate: In the province of Gour (1) there is a town, by name Konsumbee;

(1) *Gour*:—a division of the country of Bengal; formerly its capital.

in it there lived a shop-keeper, Chundun Dass. He in his old age, through the pride of wealth, married another shop-keeper's daughter, by name Lelawutee; she, through the excess of lust, in a very few days came to maturity; when that husband did not complete her happiness then she became angry. Just as the moon to one separated from his beloved, and the sun to one overcome with the heat, is not agreeable, so even to a young woman an old husband is not pleasing, because in an old man where is there strength? It is said, "As to a child medicine is not agreeable, so to her he does not seem good;" but the old man showed her infinite affection. Again it is so said, "Neither can an old man have enjoyment nor is he able to give it up: he continues longing and kissing; just as a dog without teeth on obtaining a bone can neither eat it nor let it go." When her desire was not fulfilled, then that shop-keeper's daughter Lelawutee, forsaking family respect, having no fear of religion, abandoning worldly modesty, in the excess of youth, began to commit adultery with the son of another banker, and being distracted with lust she dwelt at her father's house. Going along the road in the presence of her husband she conversed with others. It is said, "The woman who in the presence of her husband speaks words to other men, she, without doubt, becomes another's." They say, "In so many ways she becomes another's. She whose husband is a child, is old, is ugly, is of another country, is impotent, does not remain near her, shows no affection or is childless, by so many ways does that woman become an adulteress; and if she drink wine, sit in bad society, tell the faults of her husband to others, wander from house to house, sleep much, be always cleaning her body, be ever engaged in adorning herself or dwell at night in another's house, these are the defects in a woman; and she who hath no cunning, no pertness, and who speaketh not to (other) men, possesseth much modesty, that woman regard as chaste." They say, "Woman is like butter and man resembles fire, therefore for them contact is not good." Again it is said, "In infancy a father secures woman, in youth a husband guards her, in old age her son keeps her with great care. Then a woman remains virtuous, otherwise she becomes corrupt."

Afterwards one day that Lelawutee remained enjoying herself in her own house with the son of the banker, when in the mean time her husband came in from without. Seeing him coming, quickly rising from the bed and rushing before him, she embraced him. To look at him he had verily two eyes, but with one he saw not, and the one with which he saw, under pretence of kissing him on it, she put her mouth thereon and thus allowed her paramour to escape out. It is said, "Should any learn science of Jupiter himself, yet in time of adversity his understanding would not remain stable and nothing would be accomplished; but a woman would in an instant find a remedy." Then seeing Lelawutee bestowing her embraces, a bawd, comprehending the reason, reproached her and said: Do not commit such an act again. Therefore I have found out the cause of the rat jumping, that in its hole there is treasure; because without wealth there is no strength. It is said:—

COUPLET.

Gold is a hundred times more intoxicating than a thorn-apple;
Because by eating the latter one becomes mad, but by mere possession of the former insanity seizes one.

So saying the religious mendicants, joining together, extracted all the treasure out of my hole, from grief for which I have become destitute of strength, and there remained even no pleasure in my mind; because in the body whatever strength and pleasure there is, it is from wealth; and without wealth can nothing be accomplished. It is said, "A man destitute of wealth in the world is like a corpse." When I became without wealth, then from weakness I could not get along.

Then Churakurun, the holy mendicant, seeing me, said: Now this rat has been put right. Just as in the hot season a rivulet becomes without force so has he become. They say, "The understanding of one without wealth remaineth not stable; whoever possesses riches he indeed is wise, learned, prudent, generous, powerful, able, noble and clever. And without a son the house is empty; without learning a mind; and to a poor man the whole world appears empty. Again see when wealth departs, howsoever handsome one may be, yet he becomes ill-looking." Having heard such words of the Gosain (holy mendicant) then reflected I in my mind that now it is not expedient to remain here. It is said:—

COUPLET.

Incantations, conjugal affection, physic, generosity, respect, dishonor,
Secret wealth, family feud, these O Lal do not tell out openly.

Should you tell them then in vain will you lose your reputation. When the Deity is displeased then whatever penance you perform it will be fruitless. In the haughty there are two things, just as the fruit of the thorn-apple which sometimes falling on the earth dries up and sometimes ascends the forehead of Mahadeva. Therefore it is not right to contrive to live by alms. To beg from the niggard is on an equality with dying.

VERSE.

Respect and honor take their departure from the first, notwithstanding a man may be very learned and heavier than a mountain.

Says Kubidev (God of Poets) time after time he who sings praises and fillips his fingers appears more bitter (to the giver) than the Kutki.(1)

Although one may have a large person, yet (the giver) regarding him as little in his mind considers him as moveable as the cradle.

Even than grass, cotton, soum, or indeed a flower, in my opinion to beg is lighter than all.

Again Benakurun began to say to Churakurun that: He who is dependant on another for food; who gives wealth for sensual enjoyment; who is destitute of knowledge; who has his residence in a foreign land; who has a diseased body; who sleeps in another's house; living to such a man is the same as dying. It is said, "Through avarice the mind wanders; he suffers pain; he has to die; and then he loses both this world and futurity." When that holy mendicant had spoken such words, then thought I, that I am avaricious, discontented and self-inimical. Therefore has my wealth departed, and the wealth of the contented never goes. Those who being contented, are satisfied, such comfort as is theirs, such have not the dissatisfied. It is said, "Those who do not cherish avarice; who have done no one's service; who speak not supplicating words; who have not suffered the pain of separation; who have not shown impatience; from such persons wealth remains distant eight hundred miles—and the contented man has no regard for those things he possesess." Being of this opinion, I have come into this uninhabited forest, and found your heaven-like abode. They say, This world is as a tree of the objects of sense, of it they say, there are two sweet fruits, one indeed "Poetical Taste," the second "Association with the good."

Having heard so many words, Munthurk, the tortoise, said: My friend, in wealth there is great hurt: first having undergone great difficulties it is amassed, next it is preserved by exerting every effort of one's life. Such wealth, wherefore is it desirable? It is said, "Those who abandoning their own ease create wealth for others, and preserve it, they are just like porters, who die carrying burdens, and others enjoy them." Thus indeed all may be called wealthy, because it lies not in the gift or enjoyment. For this reason the poor and rich are alike; but the wealthy have one other fault,

(1) *Kutki*:—A medicinal herb or small root, called *Justicia Gauderussa*, brought from the hills, of a grey color and full of knots, bitter in taste.

that by its (riches) going they sorrow over it; this have not the poor. Again it is said, " On a man coming into the world, four things are difficult of performing—Liberality attended with mild language; divine learning without pride; valor united with mercy; abandonment of possessed wealth." Therefore store up virtue, be not over covetous, as a jackal being exceeding avaricious was slain. Heranyak said: What kind of story is that? The tortoise began to relate:

In the town of Kulliankutuk, there resided a hunter, by mame Bhairow. He one day went into the forest of Bindeachal. Having killed a deer, he was returning from thence with it on his shoulder, when, perceiving a boar coming along the road, he, being avaricious, shot an arrow at it. The arrow truly struck it, but in its dying moments it came and killed him. In the mean time, a jackal, by name Dirughrao, being hungry, happened to come there, and seeing these three lying dead there, he thought in his own mind, that I have much food, I will eat of this for some days yet, and make my body plump. Thus having reflected that jackal going close to the hunter, immediately that he began to eat the string of the bow, so soon did it break, and the point becoming loose struck him in the head, and that moment life escaped from his body. The jackal departed this life; all the flesh remained lying there. Therefore I say, that do not collect (riches) with too much eagerness, and he who, obtaining wealth, neither spends, nor gives, with him wealth remaineth so long as his life, at his death his riches and women become the purchase, truly, of another: during his life-time, continually gazing on them, he satisfies himself; at his death, they become of no use to him. Therefore, what you eat, and give away, that indeed is your own; because in this is your own self-interest and merit.

Having spoken these many words, the tortoise said to the rat: Now do not have a care for your departed treasure; because, that thing which is not attainable the wise and learned make no effort after. Therefore, my friend, do not be in any anxiety. It is said, " By studying science, all men do not become learned; those who practise it, they are truly learned. Just as by taking the name of a medicine a sick man's malady does not depart, if he eats it, then it goes; so without exertion and method wealth even is not obtained; of what use is a lamp in the hand of the blind man? Without the light of his own eyes, it will not cause light to him." Again it is said, "The teeth, hair, nails and man by leaving their places obtain no splendour, and a lion, a hero, an elephant, betel-leaf, a learned man, a virtuous man and a devotee, wheresoever they go, there, in such place, they increase their respect." They say, "As the frog in the well, and the lotus in the lake come of their own accord, so by exertion wealth comes. Ease and disquietude revolve like a wheel, and those persons who are resolute, brave, prudent, and industrious are never affected by pain." It is said, "However learned, skilful, devout, brave and opulent a man may be, yet by being covetous he incurs disrespect. The virtuous are by nature great; as if you tie round the neck of a dog a golden ornament, yet even will it appear beautiful." Therefore I say: Think not of wealth, because when the Almighty gives you a place in your mother's womb, before that, he makes manifest the milk in her breasts, and after this, birth takes place. Reflect thus:—

COUPLET:

He who made parrots green, crows black, ducks white,
Who made the peacock of variegated colors, he will think and provide for thee.

And listen! in riches there are these pains—amassing it; keeping it, and losing it; and wealth by being much increased never bestows comfort. Therefore as riches spring up, so give away and consume, for that is good; otherwise just as by placing meat aloft the birds devour it, on the ground jackals and dogs, in the water turtle and fish, within the earth worms and insects eat it, so there are four dangers in wealth—fear of the King, fear of fire, fear of thieves, fear of impostors; and in it there is also one great failing, that through desire of riches one becoming servile showeth obsequiousness, but fate cannot be averted from any one. For this reason, my friend, do not now forsake my company, during your whole life-time remain even here. It is said, "To live with contentment; to give alms; not to be angry; these are the signs of the good, they cannot proceed from the bad."

Having heard thus much, Lughuputnuk, the crow, said: Oh friend Munthurk, praise be to you, and you are worthy of being the superior of this monastery. In adversity you grant liberation, just as elephants who stick in a quagmire can be drawn out only by elephants; and in the world those men are worthy of praise who afford assistance to others in distress, and from whose door the refugee goes not disappointed, or the beggar turns not away in despair.

Having said thus much, those three began to live at that place with content and happiness, eating, drinking and sporting.

One day, at morning, an antelope, by name Chitrangad, having been frightened by a sportsman, came there; seeing him coming, Munthurk plunged into the water, the rat ran into his hole, the crow flew off and perched upon a tree; and he, looking round for some distance, perceived, that behind this one there is indeed no one, this one comes alone. Then the crow said: Brethren there is no fear, come all and sit out. Hearing this they came out and the three sat together. The antelope came near to them. Then Munthurk said: Friend, have you come in health and safety? It is said; "Of excellent persons this is the usage, that they first inquire after the welfare of those who come to their house, then showing them respect cause them to be seated, again with much politeness ask them to take food: this is the custom of excellent people." Having inquired thus much, then said he, Oh! my friend, your arrival hither how happened it? The antelope replied: Terrified by a hunter, have I come, and I am desirous of forming a friendship with you. Hiranyak said; I and you are by nature friends, and for generations past our friendship has been continued. It is said, "He who protects one in adversity is indeed a constant friend." In that you have hither come you have done well: you will remain in a better manner here than at your home.

Hearing these words the antelope took his repast, and having drunk water rested himself under a tree. Then Munthurk said; My friend, you say "that I have come from fear of the hunter;" now in this uninhabited forest where is there a hunter?

The antelope replied: in the country of Kuling, a king, Rukmangad, having conquered all the countries, has come and encamped on the bank of the river Chandrabhaga, and early in the morning he will come hither, and having cast a net into the Kurphoor lake he will catch the fish and turtle. These words having heard from the mouth of fishermen have I come, therefore it is not good to remain here. It is said, "On seeing evil coming at a distance, avert it." I have indeed told you this, but now whatever comes within your understanding that do. Munthurk said, I will go to another lake. Then the crow and antelope said: That aquatic animals acquire as much strength from water as a king from his kingdom. Then the rat Hiranyak spoke out: Friend, not indeed understanding the meaning of the words you thus think, just as a shopkeeper's son unwittingly formed a contrivance, and afterwards on beholding his wife was grieved. Munthurk said what is that story? Then the rat relates:—

There is the city of Birpoor, whose King's name was Birsein; he had a son, whose name he called Tungbul; when he arrived at manhood the

King gave the kingdom to his son. He himself began to perform his adorations of Hari(1) and the Prince to reign. One day when that King's son was returning from paying a visit to the deity, he beheld on the road the wife of some shop-keeper, young and beautiful. On beholding her beauty this one, distracted with passion, came into his own palace, and that Lawunyewutee (or with a fine complexion) on seeing the Prince, being also distracted with lust, went into her house. It is said, "To women none are dear, none are detestable, just as in the forest cows graze on new, fresh, green, verdant grass and satisfy their hearts, so does a damsel desire new and fresh lovers."

Then the Prince sent for a female messenger, and explaining to her his own condition, despatched her to her. She departing recited to her the whole state of the Prince. Then said she, I am chaste, and it is thus written for woman—"That without the permission of her lord she commit no act." For this reason, whatever my lord shall order that will I do. The bawd said: This have you well spoken, I will arrange it so. Having said thus much she came unto the King's son, and she related to him all about her. The Prince said: How will this be done? Then said the bawd, Mighty King! do not think at all about it, I will contrive it. It is said, "That work may be accomplished by a stratagem, which cannot be done by force, just as jackals by a strenuous effort slew an elephant, having got him fast in a quagmire." The King's son asked, What is that story? Then the female messenger relates:

In the forest of Brahmarunye there lived an elephant, by name Kurphoortiluck, on seeing him all the jackals began to hold a consultation, that by what means shall we slay this elephant that we may get plenty of food for four whole months. Hearing this an old jackal said, I will by stratagem slay this elephant. Having said thus much that old jackal went up to the elephant, and the traitor, with deceit working in his mind, said this unto him, Oh Deity! show kindness to me. The elephant said: Hola! Who art thou? and from whence hast thou come? He replied: all the inhabitants of these woods having assembled have sent me unto you, and have supplicating sent to say, "That in these woods we have no King, the sovereignty of the woods you take, who are the compound of every virtue." It is said, "He who is eminent in birth, joined with sobriety, splendour, justice and morality, make him a King, and if a King be good, then collect wealth and choose a wife." They say, "Just as

(1) Hari, a name of Vishnu.

living beings are dependant on rain, so also there is confidence from a King: because from fear of the King justice remains. The wife of a weak, sick, poor husband through fear of the King serves him." For this reason now make no delay, come quickly, it is not right to be lax in performing a good action. Having said this, the jackal took the elephant along with him, and the elephant also overcome with desire for sovereign dignity, accompanied him. The jackal keeping in advance, the elephant following in the rear, thus proceeded this pair. In the midst of the way, owing to the rain, it was like a quagmire; that road he took him along. Going on, the elephant stuck in the mud, then said he: Friend, now what shall I do? The jackal replied: Catch hold of my tail and come along. Having thus bid him again, when he perceived that this one is stuck fast in the midst of this, then said he, Do not make yourself uneasy, I will call and bring hither the brethren of my own race for the purpose of dragging you out. Saying thus much, calling all the jackals, he brought them there, and, under the pretence of dragging him out, they one and all tearing his hide with their teeth, devoured his flesh. The elephant after repeated shouts died.

Having recited so much the female messenger said: O great King! what cannot be accomplished by stratagem? For this reason now as I shall bid you, that do you. First then, entertain as your domestic the husband of Lawunyewutee, afterwards what I tell you that do. Hearing this the Prince entertained as a domestic Charuduut, the husband of Lawunyewutee. Then the female messenger gave the King's son instructions in the art of stratagem. Then the Prince increased his confidence in him, made him chief of all his affairs; one day the King's son said to Charuduut that: From to-day for one month I must celebrate the fast of the Holy Bhawani,(1) you must bring me a fortunate married woman.(2) On receiving the order Charuduut brought an unchaste debauched woman. Then the King's son being pure, taking her aside, having bathed her feet, caused her to partake of food, sprinkled saffron and camphor on her, placed on her clothes and ornaments, he dismissed her with great respect and honor. Then going on her road, Charuduut, being avaricious, said unto that woman that "Out of this wealth distribute some now to me." She replied, The Prince gave it to me, wherefore should I share it with you; at length she did not give him the riches. Then Charuduut reflected in

(1) Name of a Hindu Goddess, a wife of Siva or Mohadeva.

(2) This means a woman whose husband is still living.

his own mind, the King's son will give so much wealth every day for one month, for this reason, why should I not bring my own wife, that I may gratuitously carry home to my own house so much riches? Having thus reflected, he came unto his own house and said to Lawunyewutee, Oh dearest! the Prince gives so much wealth every day, if you go, then all those riches will come into our own house. Lawunyewutee said, my lord, I act according to your commands, whatever you bid me that will I consent to; at length, overcome by avarice, he brought and gave his own wife to the King's son. Then the Prince beholding her said in his mind; she to obtain whom I had entertained so great a desire, has indeed come and met me, now wherefore should I not fulfil the desire of my heart? Thus thinking, taking her apart, he fulfilled the wish of his heart, and giving her money dismissed her. Then Charuduut the shop-keeper, going unto his own house, perceiving the ornaments of his wife broken and spoilt, repented him of his own act:—

COUPLET.

Having written it in his mind, but not understanding the drift of the contrivance,
In the sight of the city-people the shop-keeper became a ridicule.

Having related thus much, the rat again said: Oh friend Munthurk, if you go from your own station to another you will then suffer affliction. Then, not heeding the rat's words, Munthurk, overcome with fear, abandoning the lake, set out for the woods, and those three accompanied him. Then going along a hunter came, and seizing hold of the tortoise bound him. They say, "When adversity comes then from having been in comfort the pain is increased, however powerful and wise a man may be yet he escapes not from adversity;" again it is even so said: "That adversity with prosperity, separation with meeting, loss with profit, defect with skill, folly with wisdom, disrespect with respect, quarrel with laughter, evil with good, these all as opportunity occurs come to pass of themselves; but fear and misfortune are the touchstones of friendship. In them the good and the bad are discovered, or else for mere talk's sake all are the friends of all:—

COUPLET.

In prosperity there are many friends: in adversity they separate themselves,
Therefore for trying the gold of friendship, adversity is made the touchstone."

Then, seeing Munthurk bound, those three began to reflect. Then said the rat to the antelope—Friend you stand before the hunter as if you were without feet. When this hunter abandoning Munthurk will run after you, then will I cut his fastenings. Again when the crow caws you escape. Hearing these words from the rat the antelope acted even so. The hunter perceived that the antelope was going limping along; I will run after and catch this one (said he): thus reflecting, having placed all his things on the edge of the water, the hunter ran after the antelope. That instant, the rat having cut the tortoise's fastenings, he fell into the water, the crow cried out, Brother escape, the Almighty has accomplished our work. Immediately on hearing this, the antelope, leaping up, ran off. The hunter in despair came back again. When he saw that not even was the tortoise there, then began he to say, "It was not right of me to act so, that I abandoned what I possessed and ran after more." It is said "great covetousness is not good," for just as I coveted the antelope, so I allowed the tortoise in my possession to escape. Thus grieving, the hunter departed from thence, these four friends thither dwelt in comfort, their heart's desire having been fulfilled.

Having related thus much, Vishnu Surma said: O mighty Princes! hearken! By hearing this story friendship is formed with the virtuous, contentment of mind is obtained, wealth increases in your house, the King follows the rules of administration and protects his subjects. This "acquisition of friends" is the first story that I have told you, for it whoever has a desire never will be deceived; ever with a clear understanding in this world will he accomplish all his undertakings; may Mohadeva grant prosperity both to the speaker and the hearer.

END OF THE FIRST STORY OF THE WHOLE COMPILATION, BY NAME "ACQUISITION OF FRIENDS."

BOOK THE SECOND.

BREACH OF FRIENDSHIP.

The Princes said to Vishnu Surma, O Holy Preceptor! we have heard the narrative regarding the Acquisition of Friends; now, showing favor towards us, tell us the second story on the Breach of Friendship.

Then Vishnu Surma said, O Princes! First a jackal formed a friendship between a bullock and a tiger, and afterwards caused it to be killed by the tiger. Then the Princes said what is that story? Then Vishnu Surma began to relate it:

That in the Southern territories there was a city called Suburna, where a shop-keeper resided, Burdman by name, who was very wealthy; on a certain day, seeing the wealth of another shop-keeper, he thought within himself; "If I can in any way collect more wealth it will be well." It is said, "Whose heart does not become jealous on seeing another more powerful, wealthy and learned than himself? And in the same manner who does not become proud at beholding the increase of his own wealth? because every one respects the wealthy." Again it is thus said, "That wealth itself leaves the irresolute and idle: as a young woman has no desire for an old man, so neither has wealth for them. The Almighty never exalts those who being idle sit at home contented." It is said, "May Bhugwan never give an irresolute son to any one." Again they say, "That thing which is not to be found (is scarce) if you exert yourself will be obtained, (or that of which you are not yet possessed if you exert yourself you will obtain.) If you give no thought to it you will then not get it. Having thus considered, the shop-keeper began again to say within himself: Of what use is that wealth which you neither spend yourself nor give away? If having power you do not slay your enemy, of what use the having that power? And if having learned science, you know not what is right, of what advantage is that knowledge? Again, if having a body you are not a benefactor, and do not subdue the passions, what is the use of that body? It is said, "Wealth increases by a little and little exertion, so also an earthern pot fills by water dropping drop after drop; and he who takes breath (lives) without knowledge and wealth, him consider like the bellows of a blacksmith."

Having thus considered, Burdman, the shop-keeper, having yoked Nunduk and Sunjewuk in his car, and loading it with immense wealth and property, mounted his car and went towards Cashmere. It is said, "What is the weight to a powerful man? and to a merchant where is there any strange country? To a sweet-spoken man who is an enemy?" When he had gone half way, the foot of Sunjewuk breaking in the midst of the great forest called Doorghe, he staggered and fell down. Seeing it fall, the merchant began to say, "Whatsoever plans one may form, yet the fruit (fulfilment of them) is in the hands of the Almighty." Thinking thus, and leaving the bullock there, the merchant proceeded onwards. The bullock remained there. In a few days, from eating fresh grass and drinking clean water, it became very strong, and once, being very happy, bellowed. In that place a tiger, called Pingal, reigned, but no one had conferred on him the mark of sovereignty. It is said, "The lion on account of his strength is called the King of beasts." The tiger had gone at that very time to the banks of the Jumna to drink water. Going there, and hearing the sound of Sunjewuk's bellowing, being terrified in mind, without drinking water, he returned to his abode. There two jackals, Dumnuk and Kurtuk, resided. On seeing this event, Dumnuk said to Kurtuk; Friend, did you see anything? What is the reason that the tiger going to-day to the banks of the Jumna, without drinking water returned to his abode, and remains thoughtful? Kurtuk replied; Friend, it is my opinion, that there is no need of asking regarding one whom you do not serve. They say, "What is the use of asking the road where you have not to go?" Now to serve him I am ashamed, but I do so through covet of provender. It is said, "He who wishes for wealth, by serving, sells his body in the hands of others; and consider as imperfect the devotion of those who undergo hunger, thirst, heat, cold and wet for others: because to the servile and dependant to live and die are equivalent."

VERSE.

They say, "It is well to give in a good way, and it is also good not to give even a little in a bad way. It is better for your house to remain empty, than to make friends with the bad. Associate with the lowest of the good, but forsake the chief of the ignorant. It is easy to discern the intent of the good, but fear the kindness of the wicked. Be content with the small profit of a merchant, but forsake the great gain of gaming. Having fallen into good society, accomplish your undertaking by your own exertions. Rather acknowledge yourself in the wrong, than quarrel with the low. Give all you have, but be not dependant on or under the power of any one. That man is called dead, whose master does not like him, and says, get away from this, and remain not here. By showing for him such contempt he destroys his character; nevertheless the ignorant remains dependant for the sake of wealth. As a courtesan adorns herself for the sake of a strange man, so an ignorant man, by acquiring a little knowledge, becomes the dependant of another."

Therefore in my opinion, there is no fool in the world like a servant. Dumnuk said; Friend, say not this. It is said, "Serve a good master with great care, by which you may obtain the wish of your heart. If you serve you will obtain the royal umbrella, (1) fly-flapper, an elephant, a horse, &c. and all the blessings (appertaining unto) of wealth; and if you serve not, then where will you obtain all these?" Therefore it is incumbent to serve. Again Kurtuk said; Friend, what need have we of what you make mention? It is said, "Without consideration and reflection if you intermeddle, you will die as died the monkey." Dumnuk said: What like is that story? Then Kurtuk relates:—

(1) These all are insignia of royalty or wealth.

In the Mugudh(1) country there was a Kaeth(2), named Shubh Dutt, who had commenced the formation of an arena for sport, in the midst of the forest of Dhurmarun. There, a carpenter having sawn wood, and placed a wedge therein, went away on some business. A monkey of the forest, in his wantonness, and doomed to die, catching hold of the wedge sat upon the wood, and his parts hung in the cleft of the wood. When in his wantonness he contrived to extract the wedge, that instant, as he pulled it out, his parts became jammed, and he died. Therefore I say; Without self-interested motives do not exert yourself. Dumnuk said: He who is chief does everything; for a servant to think thus is not proper. Kurtuk replied; Brother, to forsake your own work, and to meddle in that of others is not right, and if you should intermeddle then it will be as the poor ass, who was killed by interfering in another's business. Dumnuk said: What is that story? Then Kurtuk relates:—

In the city of Barunusi, there was a certain washerman, named Kurpoorpat, who had married a young wife, and with whom one day, at night, after amusing themselves, he was lying in a deep sleep. Thieves entered his house, and in their yard there was an ass and a dog. The ass, seeing the thieves, said to the dog: Holloa! It is thy business that thou awake thy master. The dog replied: Oh! make no mention of my duty. What! dos't thou not know, that he gives me nothing to eat? It is said, "The master has no respect for his servant till adversity befals him." Then said the ass: Listen, oh mad one! what kind of servant is he, who makes a request in time of need? The dog replied: What kind of master is he, who approves of his servant when he requires him? The son and servant are alike. It is proper for the master to feed and clothe them. The ass said: Thou art a sinner, in that thou performest not thy master's work: and my name is Swamibukht, (a follower of my lord). Therefore, so that my master may awake, that plan will I adopt. Again, the dog said: Oh endure (the heat of) the sun by turning your back to it; placing fire before you, warm yourself, and in the presence of your master and in his absence be pure. But this master is not such an one; and if thou put thy foot (interfere) in my affairs, then may my silence affect thee. Hearing his words, the ass receded from thence, and going close up to the washerman, and placing his mouth to his ear, brayed. Then that washerman, starting

(1) Country including Patna, Gya, &c.

(2) Name of a Hindu tribe.

up from sleep, being enraged, struck him with an iron club. From that blow he died.

Therefore, I say, never meddle with the rights of another. It is our duty to search for food; but to-day we have not a care about that: because from yesterday's flesh a great quantity remains. With it we for many days will fill our bellies, by partaking of it. Dumnuk said: If you serve merely for food then it is not right. The service of a King is even thus: For one's self-interest, and that of others; for by serving him, you may assist your virtuous friend, and destroy your wicked enemy. This desire remaineth in the mind. One does not merely serve for the sake of filling one's belly. It is said, "That in the world, he on whom relying many people live, his life is fruitful." All servants are not alike; in each and every servant there is a great difference. For instance, one is dear at five cowries (1), and one is not to be had for a lac of rupees. They say, "A horse, an elephant, wood, stone, clothes, woman, man and grain, in the value of each one of these, there is a great difference. See a dog, if he gets a little flesh hanging round a bone, then remaineth he satisfied therewith; and before the lion stands the jackal, then even the lion leaving him will kill the elephant." Therefore I say: "That those who are noble do noble deeds." Again, when the dog wags his tail and shows his belly, then he gets a morsel, and the elephant tied in a shed after much contrivance, with infinite condescension, takes his provender. It is said, "In the world, with wisdom, power, renown and pride, to live one hour is well: but without respect, like the crow, eating dung, to live many days, of what avail is it? If one lives satisfying one's inward cravings, between that man and a beast what difference is there?" Then Kurtuk replied: In no way are you and I the servants of this King. Again Dumnuk said: Brother, watching an opportunity endeavour to become a minister. A large stone is with great difficulty raised, but to let it fall is easy: and contrive your own celebrity to keep ever fresh. Then Kurtuk inquired; Brother, do you know aught why the tiger was this day frightened? Dumnuk replied; Brother, in this what is there to discover? A learned man knows by guess without being told; or if one be told, then would a beast know. But that which a man approves, is to him agreeable. In my opinion in the service of the King one should remain, and when the King calls out: Is any one there? then to answer: My lord what are your commands? thy servant awaits them; in that manner, whenever he may call out thus, in this same manner to answer

(1) A cowrie is a small shell used as a coin.

him: If he say aught, you should ever remain on the alert to catch the words: never disobey his orders; for one instant, never leave his company; but like his shadow, to him ever keep close. Kurtuk said; Friend, It is said, "Out of season, unto the King, should any go, he would reap dishonor." Dumnuk replied; Yet for all this, the servant should not forsake his master. It is said, "Not to exert oneself for fear of the world, and not to eat for fear of indigestion, is the act of a coward. Howsoever ignoble, defiled and ignorant a man may be, if near the King he remain, the King shows friendship towards him." They say, "That fire, a woman, the King and the creepers, always attach themselves to what is near them, there is no doubt of this." Kurtuk said: Will you ask the King why he was afraid? He replied; I will first go and see the King whether he is pleased or sad. Kurtuk said: How will you know that? Again he replied, Consider that master pleased who is gladdened by seeing his servant at a distance coming towards him, who speaks to him, reckons him among his own servants, shows him great kindness on seeing a little of his work, and increases his respect for him daily: and look on that King as displeased, who, on seeing his servant coming to him, turns away his eye, allows him to entertain hopes of a gift to-day or to-morrow, does not give a thought to his words, and finds out defects in his good qualities. Therefore do not think more of this; I will speak as I find the King. It is said, "That he who is a sapient minister, makes justice apparent from oppression, and prosperity from adversity." Again Kurtuk said; Brother, even Jupiter himself would be dishonored, were he to speak out of season: what need is there then to mention man? Then Dumnuk said; Friend, do not fear, I will not speak out of season. It is said, "The friend of any one who goes astray, will not remain without speaking to him," what kind of counsellor is he, who does not give his counsel in due season, or out of it? because greatness is obtained when occasion offers.

COUPLET.

Having lost the opportunity every one afterwards repents.
Neither the one nor the other remains (opportunity or repentance) but the mere mention of it by the public.

Having spoken thus much, Dumnuk again said; Now I will do whatever you tell me. Kurtuk replied; Do whatever you think is for your good. Hearing this, Dumnuk went to Pingul the King: making his obeisance and joining his hands, he stood before him. Then the King laughing said: Dumnuk, it is a long time since you last came to me. Saying this, he seated him. Then Dumnuk, finding out the inward feelings of the King, knowing him to be frightened, said thus: O Lord of the earth, there is no business between you and me, but I am a servant, it is expedient that I should come at all times; because one time or other grass becomes of use to clean the teeth and ears. Therefore if a servant does not become useful, in season or out of it, then of what use is he? Although it is a long time since you asked of me advice, yet my wisdom is not decreased. It is said "If you tie a jewel on the foot, and sapphire on the head, the sapphire remains sapphire, and the jewel, a jewel. He is really learned whose wisdom remains stable though he be disgraced." Therefore, O great King, it is right you should always be discreet. There are three descriptions of persons in the world—good, indifferent and bad. Entrust an undertaking to one as you find him, and ascertain the services of a domestic. If the King values not the services of his servant, the servant will remain much distressed. Therefore, O great King, an ornament and a servant receive splendour according to where they should be. If the King act according to the advice of his minister, many servants will come. It is said "That if a horse, a weapon, science, musical instruments, a man and a woman be in the possession of the good, then they remain well, and bad in the hands of the bad." Again it as said, "If a King shows unkindness to (the wise) those of a good understanding, they will not remain near him, and if the wise do not remain near him, then justice flies, and when justice is gone, then the people are distressed; but if the King show kindness all will obey him. Good words are pleasing to all, but to speak softly is very difficult."

When Dumnuk had uttered these words, then the King said: O Dumnuk! you being the son of my minister never come to me, I did not think you to be so. How have you come now? Dumnuk replied: O great King! I have come to ask you something; if I obtain your permission then will I ask it. The tiger replid: Dumnuk, ask me without hesitation. Dumnuk said: O great King! what is the reason that having gone to the banks of the river, without drinking water, being thoughtful, you returned to your abode? Kindly tell me this, that the doubt of my mind may be removed. The tiger said: O brother, I never tell the secrets of my mind to any one; but as you are the son of my minister I tell you, but do not repeat them to any one. It is this: To-day when I went to drink water, I heard a dreadful noise, through fear of which I fled from thence, and came and laid down here, and am thinking in my mind that some very powerful animal has come into this forest. Therefore if I go and dwell in another forest it will be better for me; to live here is not expedient. Hearing this, Dumnuk said: O great King, I am at a loss how to explain it. Ever since I heard that sound I have been trembling through fear; but it is not proper that the minister should first cause the King to forsake his abode, or excite him to fight. Again it is incumbent on the King to ascertain the merits of the following, in adversity: a servant, a wife, wisdom and power; because adversity is their touchstone. The tiger said: I have a great fear in my mind. Then Dumnuk said within himself, if you were not afraid why would you converse with me? Reflecting thus in his mind he again said: O incarnation of faith, as long as I live, fear not at all in the least. I will call and bring Kurtuk, &c. and all the servants. It is thus written in Moral Philosophy, that, "In the time of adversity the King summoning all his attendants, asking their advice and making them unanimous should entrust the affairs of the state to them." Saying this Dumnuk called Kurtuk, and introduced him to the King. Then the King dressing them in robes of honor, giving them betel, (1) dismissed them for the purpose of removing his fear. Afterwards going along the road, Kurtuk said to Dumnuk; Brother, you have not acted well in taking the reward of the King without thinking. How do you know whether we shall be able to remove that fear or not? It is said, "Without considering, never take the things of another; but especially do not take the reward of the King; because if the affair be never accomplished, the King gets angry, and you do not know what distress he may subject you to." It is thus said also, "That wealth dwells in the favor of the King, and renown in his power, and death in his anger. The glory of all the deities is in the King; therefore if a man remains under the orders of the King it is good; because the lord of the earth, of a human form, is one of the great deities." Again Dumnuk said; Friend, you remain silent, I know the cause of all this; that he has been frightened on hearing the sound of the bull's bellowing, and I also can kill the bull. What injury can he do to the tiger? Again Kurtuk said; Brother, if such be the case, then why not by telling the King remove all fear from his mind. Dumnuk replied; Friend, if I had told this to the King at first, then how would I and you have obtained situations. It is said, "That servants should never keep their

(1) Given when one person undertakes to perform the work of another which is called बीरा उठाना. The meaning of Bira is a betel-leaf made up with a preparation of the areca nut, spices and lime.

masters free from care; if they do so, then they will be like Dudhikurun the male-cat. Hearing this, Kurtuk said; What is that story? Then Dumnuk relates:—

There lived a tiger, named Maha Bikram, in a cave of the mountain called Urbad. When he slept there, then a mouse, coming out of his hole, used to nibble his hair. When he awoke, he would escape into his hole. It is said, "Little foes are not killed by the great." Observing the wickedness of the mouse, the tiger thought within himself: "That if I bring any one equal to him, then he will be killed; otherwise I will not be able to sleep owing to him." Considering this, going into the village, he brought with great courtesy, a male-cat, named Dudhikurun, and kept him. The cat used to sit at the entrance of the cave, and, through fear of the cat, the mouse did not come out of his hole, and the tiger slept comfortably. Therefore the tiger, through fear of the mouse, greatly esteemed the cat. At length, after some days, finding an opportunity, the cat killed and eat the mouse. When the tiger heard not the sound of the mouse, then he considered in his mind; "That business is accomplished for the which I brought the cat. Now what need is there to keep the cat. Thus considering, the tiger ceased to give him food. Then the cat, dying with hunger in that place, fled from thence. Therefore I say, never keep the master free from care.

Having said thus, Dumnuk seating Kurtuk on a lofty place, under a tree, and leaving some jackals with him, went himself alone to Sunjewuk and said; From whence have you come? When he had related to him all his former circumstances, then Dumnuk said: The King of this forest is a tiger. How do you live here? Then being terrified, the bullock said; You by some means or other render me assistance. Again Dumnuk, on his part, making him fearless, said; My elder brother, Kurtuk, is the King's minister. I will first introduce you to him, afterwards I will cause an interview between you and the King. Thus having spoken, Dumnuk taking that bullock unto Kurtuk, threw him at his feet. Then Kurtuk, stroking the back of the bullock, said; Now in this wood, without fear, graze and stroll about, and have no kind of care in your mind. Thus having removed his fear, taking him with him they came and sat at the royal gate. It is said, "Wisdom is greater than force, see without force an elephant by skill can be brought into subjection." Again Kurtuk said to Sunjewuk; Now you remain here till I go and return from the King; then I will take you to him. Having said this, those two (Dumnuk and Kurtuk) both went unto the King, and making their reverential salutation, with joined hands, remained standing in his presence. Then the King, with soft words, enquired of them, that they should tell him the news of the undertaking for which they had set out. Then Dumnuk, joining his hands, lowering his head, began to relate it :—

O Sire, (said he) I have seen him, he is very powerful, but after what we said to him, he desires to meet with you. We will bring him immediately, but you sit on your guard. Be not terrified by his sound, consider the cause of the sound: just as by ascertaining the reason of a noise a bawd obtained greatness. The King asked what is that story? Then Dumnuk relates :—

On Sreepurbut there is a town called Brihmpoor, and on the summit of that mountain an evil spirit, named Ghuntakurn, resided, of which all the inhabitants of the city were aware; because they used always to hear his voice. One day a thief having stolen the bell from the city, was going with it to that mountain, when a tiger there killed and eat him, and that bell fell into the hands of a monkey; when he used to ring it, then the inhabitants of the city thought that the demon was roaming about. One day one of them returned, having seen that dead man, and he told every one how Ghuntakurn having become incensed, has commenced eating men: this I have seen with my own eyes. Having heard his words, through fear, the people of the city began to fly. Then a bawd, by name Kurahya, finding out of the cause of the bell ringing, went to the King and said: O Sire, give me something, then having slain Ghuntakurn I will return. Hearing this the King gave her (1,00,000 Rs.) a lac of rupees, and dismissed her for the purpose of killing him. Then the money she put bye in her house, and taking a great many edibles with her, she took the road to the forest. Going thither she saw that a monkey perched up on a tree was ringing the bell. On seeing it, this one scattered all the eatables on a mound. That monkey immediately on seeing them, jumping down from the tree came thither, beholding the bread, sweatmeats, fruits and roots, he threw down the bell, as he stretched out his hand to eat, the bell became loosed. Then the bawd taking the bell went her way, coming to the city she gave it into the hands of the King, and said: Your excellency, I have returned from killing him. Hearing this, and seeing the bell, the King showed her great respect, and the city people adored her.

Therefore I say: Do not be frightened by a mere sound, O Sire, first think over the cause of it, then lay your plans. This is the conveyance of the divine Shiva (1) and you that of Parwuti; therefore knowing this to be your abode he is bellowing fearlessly. It is expedient for you to advance to meet him, and welcoming him to serve him; because to-day he is your guest. By your attendance on him, Ishwur (2) and Parwuti will be pleased. Hearing this, the tiger said to Dumnuk: You, treating him with politeness, introduce him to me; he indeed is my brother. Then Dumnuk introduced the bullock Sunjewuk to the tiger Pingul. They both experienced great comfort at meeting, and after a few days, great friendship sprung up between them.

Again one day Sitkurun, by name, a tiger, brother of the King, came thither. Then Sunjewuk exclaiming said, O great King! where is the flesh of the deer you have killed to-day? The tiger replied: Brother, Kurtuk and Dumnuk know. Then Sunjewuk said: O great King! well then, just ask them is it here or not? Again the tiger replied; This is my custom that whatever I bring, that I give away. Then Sunjewuk said: O great King! it is not right for a minister to expend what comes, nor is it the custom without the permission of the King to give to any one. It is said: "Against adversity keep wealth," and a minister should be such that he collect the King's wealth, expend a little and save up much. The King's treasure is like life; every one for the sake of money serves the King. If you become without wealth, even the wife of your home will not obey you. Why need we mention others? In this world wealth indeed has the supremacy. Whoever has wealth is great. These are defects in a minister: If he expend much; protect not the subjects; if by acts of oppression and injustice he fill the treasury, and tells falsehoods in the presence of the King; then in a few days, the kingdom will assuredly fall, because without thought and reflection if a work be performed, that work never stands. When Sunjewuk had spoken these words, Sitkurun said; Brother, in that you have invested these jackals with power and authority you have done well: but I have heard from old people that Brahmins, Chutrees, relatives, benefactors and friends you should not entrust with the affairs of your kingdom. For if the Brahmin squander away his wealth, the King cannot punish (3) him, and the Chutree on attaining power, then would he snatch away the king-

(1) Shiva, or Mohadeva, is represented riding a bull, and his wife Parwuti on a tiger.

(2) Is a name for Shiva.

(3) The only punishment for a Brahmin doing anything wrong is to send him out of the city.

dom: Again the relative would never obey orders; the benefactor would consider all (wealth) as nothing; and the friend would consider himself equal with the King. Therefore to these persons never entrust your kingdom. Again it is thus said "That you should not hastily remove your minister from office: gently and quietly squeeze him, just as clothes after being washed are wrung." When he (Sitkurun) had thus alarmed him (Pingul) then suspicion also arose in his mind. They say, "The courtesan, whose wife is she? and the King, whose friend is he?"

VERSE:

Is the snake well disposed, the tiger merciful, the crow pure, and the gambler true?
Is the fire cold, stone soft, the night of the change of the moon light?
Is the coward resolute, the courtezan chaste, what, O ignorant one, can a drunkard be wise?
Moteeram says; O wise! listen, who has ever seen or heard of the friendship of a King?

Then the King said: Brother, you speak the truth. These two do not obey my orders, and give me trouble. Again Sitkurun said: Brother, it is said "Reputation is lost by hauteur, wisdom by bad desire, wealth by idleness, family by bad action, justice by avarice." Again it is thus said:

COUPLET.

He who disobeys the King's orders and shows disrespect to Brahmins; and that woman who has a separate bed from her husband, regard as slain without weapons.

And such is morality, that if his son disobey him, that the King give him punishment. Again, that he protect his subjects from the thief and avaricious minister, and cherish them in the same way as he would his son. And listen, Brother, to-day I have eaten your food (am your guest) therefore for your good am I speaking. This Sunjewuk is very virtuous, pure-minded and the mine of good works; therefore if your own good you desire, invest him with power and authority. The King hearing these words from his brother, made Sunjewuk his minister, and took the government away from Dumnuk and Kurtuk. Then Dumnuk said to Kurtuk; Friend, now what shall we do? This fault is of our own committing. As by touching the picture Kundurupketu, and by coveting the jewel, the merchant, and by his acts, the messenger, all reaped distress, so indeed have we received the reward of our deeds. Then Kurtuk said: What is that story? So Dumnuk thus relates:

In Kanchunpoor there was a King, named Bekramadith, whose servants were taking away a barber to kill him. There a mendicant said to the King's servants, this barber has committed no crime. The servants replied: Tell us his history. Then the mendicant said: First, how my own faults effected me, so listen thereto: "I am the son of Jambooketu, King of Sunguldeep, and my name is Kundurupketu. One day a trader came to my city, and brought for inspection to me very great rarities. When I asked him, Where did you get these? Then he began to relate, saying: O great King, we merchants go to the sea-shore for traffic, where annually a tree springs up from the sea. On it a very beautiful maiden, decorated with ornaments, set with jewels, a damsel being seated, sends forth great rarities, and merchants and traders take them, and travelling from country to country sell them. When he had spoken thus much to me, then I, taking him with me, went to the sea-shore, and going there, immediately on seeing her, I jumped into the sea; on jumping in, a golden house came in sight. Then I, getting up, ran into it. Seeing me, she sent a messenger, who proceeding on (at length) came to me. I asked her who is this (damsel)? She replied: She is the daughter of Kundurupketu, the King of the demi-gods, and her name is Rutunmunjuri. Hearing these words, I advanced onwards, and going near to her experienced great delight. Then said she: O Lord, as is best pleasing to yourself remain here; but never touch this drawn picture of the demi-gods. Then after having married (1) her I remained there some days. One day, not acting up to her injunctions, as I touched that picture, she instanter gave me such a kick, that I went and fell in the Mugudh country. Since that day, in her absence from me, having become a mendicant, I wander about. To-day having come into your city during the night, I remained in the house of a cow-herd; so there I saw that the cow-herd on beholding his wife conversing with her gallant, getting angry, tied her to a pillar, and that being intoxicated he went to sleep. When half the night was spent, then the wife of a barber, a bawd, coming up to her, said: O hearken you, in your absence that poor wretch is dying. Taking compassion on him I have come unto you; now make no delay, having tied me to this pillar go, and having made him happy, return. Having heard these words she did so. Then the cow-herd awoke, and began to say to her (2): Now why do you not go unto your gallant? When she made no rejoinder, then he cut off her nose, and, being intoxicated with wine, he again slept. In the mean time the cow-herdess returning inquired of the barber's wife saying, Sister! Is all well? She replied: You have returned well, but here I have lost my nose. Hearing this the cow-herdess became herself bound, and she dismissed the barber's wife. When the barber's wife had gone to her own house then the

(1) गंधर्वविवाह is the word used, meaning a kind of marriage.

(2) The barber's wife, whom he mistook for his own wife.

cow-herd again awoke, and whatever words came into his mouth those began he to utter. At that time the cow-herdess said; You are my lord, beat, tie me, do whatever you like; but who is there such that would cast reproach on me. My actions and virtues, the supporters of the eight regions; the moon, the sun, the earth, the heavens, the fire, the water the wind, the night, the day and the two lights know: and whatever act an animate being commits, of it to them there is knowledge. Now I speak by my virtue and chastity, O deity sun! that if I abide by my virtue and chastity, then may my nose not appear cut to the public. Hearing these words, the cow-herd, going close up to her, perceived that her nose was every whit whole as before. Immediately on beholding it he fell at her feet and said: Pardon me my offence, I have oppressed you without fault. Then she, embracing him, said: O lord, in this there was no fault of yours, this is the fruit of my destiny. Then again the barber's wife returning to her own home, sat with her nose in her hand. When on the day dawning her husband asked for the shaving case, she gave a razor into his hand. He getting angry threw it in her direction. Then she exclaimed aloud, Ha! This merciless one has struck my nose with a razor. Hearing her exclamation, you without thought or reflection have seized and brought him, and are taking him away to kill him: but he is not in fault. And with me is this virtuous merchant, listen unto his story; that this one for twelve years in a foreign country having earned wealth, taking it, was returning to his own home, when coming into this city, he put up during the night in the house of a bawd. That common woman, having fashioned a wooden image, placed springs in it, and fastened a jewel on its head, had placed it at her door. This virtuous one, struck with avarice, getting up in the middle of the night, going near to the image, stretched out his hand, and as he was about to take the gem that instant the spring flew open. His two hands became fast. Catching the sound of the spring flying open, that wanton one coming up to him said: From Mulayagir (1) the necklace of pearls that you have brought, so give it to me, otherwise early in the morning you will have to go to the Chief of the Police, and you will not return alive from thence. Hearing these words of hers, this one, being terrified, gave her all his wealth and came and joined me. Hearing these words from the mendicant, the servants of the King having come to a decision, and letting him (the barber) go,

(1) Mulayagir, or Mulagir, is a mountain, or range of mountains, from which the best sandal wood is brought, answering to the Western Ghats in the Peninsula of India.

causing the courtezan to refund to the merchant his wealth, and awarding to each a suitable punishment, let them all loose. Therefore I say; That as those suffered distress from their own fault, so have we reaped the reward of our own deeds. But, Brother Kurtuk, now what has happened, has happened: but do not think over it: Listen, as I formed friendship between these two, so will I now excite enmity. It is said, "Those who are cunning, they cause falsehoods to appear as truths," just as a cow-herdess turning falsehood into truth, in the very sight of her lord, caused the escape of her gallant from the house. Kurtuk said what is that story? Then Dumnuk relates:—In the town of Dwarika there was a cow-herd's wife, an adulteress. She remained with the Chief of Police and his son. One day, at night time, she remained in sexual enjoyment with the son of the Chief of Police. In the mean time the Chief of Police coming, called out at the door. Then she hid his son in an apartment and opened the door, and afforded him pleasure; after this her husband came. Then she taught the Chief of Police this lesson, saying "I am going to open the door, but you placing your club over your shoulder, getting angry, go out of the house. Then afterwards I will concoct something. He did accordingly. Then the cow-herd, coming into the house, said unto his wife: "To-day the Chief of Police from my house wherefore did he incensed go forth? The cow-herdess replied: Why did the Chief of Police leave our house angry? His son, being vexed with him, came and concealed himself in my house; so he desires from me his son. In the mean time in that you came, seeing you he went away. Having said thus, the cow-herdess brought the son of the Chief of Police out of the apartment, and said to him: Entertain no fear, I am going to put you out; go where you can find shelter (1). Having thus said, she put him out of the house. It is said:—

COUPLET.

Of an appetite two-fold that of men, understanding four-fold, desire eight-fold, cunning six-fold; in this manner are all women."

Therefore I say, when occasion arises, whosesoever's wisdom is effective, he is learned. Again Kurtuk said; Brother, between those two there is great friendship, how will you cause a breach? Then Dumnuk replied: Friend, work which can be performed by stratagem cannot be achieved by force. As a snake was killed by a crow, so will I cause this one to be slain. Kurtuk said: What is that story? Then Dumnuk relates:—

(1) Literally "Go wherever your horns can find room."

In the northern country is a mountain, by name Bidhiadhur. There, on the top of a certain tree, a male and female crow remained, and at the root of the same a (black) snake. When the female crow gave eggs, then the snake, climbing up the tree, would take and eat them, and through desire for the eggs, daily, he, climbing the tree, would go and lie in the hollow. When the female again became pregnant, then she said to the crow; O Husband! forsaking this tree if we go and dwell elsewhere, it will be well, because it is said, "He whose wife is bad, friend deceitful, servant one who gives saucy answers, and whose house is a dwelling for snakes, without doubt will meet with his death." For which reason it is not expedient to remain here. The crow replied, O beloved! now do not fear, because I have borne with many of this snake's offences, but now I will not bear with them more. The female said, What will you do to this? The crow replied; Beloved, that work which can be performed with stratagem, cannot be achieved by force. As a hare through cunning killed a very powerful tiger, so I will not leave this one till I have slain him. The female inquired; What is that story? Then the crow relates:—

On the mountain Mandara (1) dwelt a tiger named Durdunt. He used to kill a great many beasts. One day all the beasts of the forest assembling, having reflected, said one to the other; This tiger daily comes and devours one beast and kills many. Therefore going unto him let us promise to give him one beast, and let each in his turn convey one to him, then will it be well. Thus having conversed among themselves, they went unto the tiger, and, joining their hands, making a reverential salutation, stood before him according to rank. Seeing them, the tiger said: What do you want? They replied, O Lord! You go daily in search of food, you slay many, and devour few. Therefore this is our request: that for your eating we may daily convey one beast to you and return, do not you take trouble yourself. He said: Very good. Thus did they return, having given their word to the tiger. After this, whosoever's turn came, he used to go, and he would eat him. In this manner, after some days (had past), the turn of a very aged hare came. Then thus he thought within himself. That my body is small, with it his belly will not be filled. Then he will devour more of my brethren; so that in a turn or two he will make an end of our race. Therefore, if in my own

(1) Mandar, or Mandara, a famous mountain in India, with which the ocean was churned.

life time I destroy this one, then well will it be. Thus reflecting he arose from his abode. Moving slowly on, he arrived near to the tiger. Then he seeing him getting angry, said, Holloa! Why have you come so late? Again the hare, joining his hands in supplication, addressed these words to him. O Lord! It is no fault of mine, I was coming along to you, in the road I met with another tiger. He said to me, Ho! Whither are you going? I replied: That I am going unto my master. He said: Of this forest I am verily the lord, other lords from whence have they come hither? Again I said: That previous to this day I have never seen you. On hearing thus much, he, getting angry, kept me seated, then said I to him, "It is not right in a servant that he tarry in his master's work, you have detained me, this my master will not know. Moreover he will regard my words as false, and will say in his own mind: That this one, going unto his home, has remained asleep, and coming to me speaketh falsehoods. Therefore do not detain me. I will go and come from my master, he will be looking out for me. I go giving you this my word, that having spoken with my master, I will quickly retrace my steps." On my saying these words, having bound me to my word, he dismissed me, then came I unto you. Lord! In this there is no fault of mine.

Having heard these words, the tiger said, Ho! In my forest another tiger, from whence has he come? You show him to me immediately; without slaying him, I will not take food to-day. Thus having conversed, they both set out from thence; the hare in advance, the tiger following in the rear. When after proceeding on they arrived at some distance in the forest, then the hare, going near to a well, stood still, then said the tiger, Ho! he who detained thee, where is he? The hare replied, O Lord! that one, through fear of you, has entered this well. Hearing this much, the tiger, being enraged, went to the edge of the well, and as he looked into the water, then his own image appeared in it. Beholding his reflection, he immediately jumped into the water, and died by drowning. Then the hare returning to his own abode, told to all the dwellers of the forest, that I have come from slaying the tiger, I have removed afar your distress for generations. Hearing this all the dwellers of the forest showered down blessings upon him. Having related thus much, the male said to the female crow, O beloved! see, the work which was performed through stratagem, could not have been achieved by force. Then the female said, Lord! that in which there is good, that devise. The crow, then flying from thence, proceeding on, saw that a King's son, having placed on the bank of a certain tank, his clothes, missiles and weapons, was bathing therein. This one took and flew off with his pearl necklace, and going into his hollow, and throwing that necklace on to the neck of the snake, went and sat apart. Pursuing after him, the servants of the King, seeing him, came on. When they saw not the necklace in the beak of the crow, then one of their number climbed up the tree. He perceived, that, in the hollow lay a black snake, with the necklace on. Seeing this, that servant of the King reflected in his own mind, that the necklace truly I behold, but without forming some plan, it will not come into my hands. I must contrive for this. Saying thus much, having killed the snake with arrows, he brought and gave the necklace to the King's son. Therefore I say, Brother, by stratagem what cannot be achieved?

Again Kurtuk said, Brother, whatever you think expedient that do. Then Dumnuk rising from thence, having gone unto the tiger Pingul, he said, O great King! Although I have no business with you, yet in season and out of season it is expedient for us to come unto you. It is said that "When a King treadeth in an evil path, then it is right for the servant that he give warning unto the King, and if he do not warn him, then the reputation of the servant goes, whether afterwards the King regards, or does not heed, yet it is right to tell him. Sire, a King is formed for enjoyment, and a servant to perform service." Again it is said, "If a King's Kingdom is ruined, then the blame rests with the minister: no one would say aught against the King." Therefore it is expedient for the minister, that he suffer hardship in the performance of his master's service, and give up his wealth and life: but that he let not go the kingdom, and if a minister sees the affairs of the kingdom going wrong, and does not apprize the King, what kind of a minister is he? And if a King, in season or out of season (at all times), does not hearken unto the words of his servant, then what kind of master is he? Pingul said: What are you desirous of saying? Tell me. Dumnuk began to say, O Lord of the Earth! this Sunjewuk casts reproach upon you, and says, that: Now this King has become void of greatness, it is expedient to protect the subjects. From these words, your excellency, such falls within my comprehension, that now he himself wishes to govern. Hearing these words, the King remained silent. Again Dumnuk said: O incarnation of faith! you have appointed such a powerful minister, that without asking you your advice in the affairs of the state, all at once, he himself, begins to rule: this is not right. Just as Chanuk, the minister, slew the King, may it never be so (with you.) The King inquired of him, What is that story? Then Dumnuk relates:—

In a certain country there was a King, by name Nunduk. His minister's name was Chanuk. Well, the King having delivered over to that minister the reins of Government, being himself free from all anxiety, began to enjoy himself, and the minister to reign. One day, that King, taking the minister with him, went out hunting. Going into the forest, he perceived a stag. They galloped their horses after it: then other people pressed on their's, but none of their horses could catch up their two, then, one and all, lagging, fell in the rear, and those two proceeded on. When the stag, bounding out of their reach entered the forest, then the King, overcome indeed with heat and thirst, alighting from his horse, sat down under a tree. At length that King getting the minister to hold his horse, being overcome by thirst, set out from thence in search of water. After having gone some distance, looking about, then a tank full of pellucid water came in view; immediately on beholding it, being delighted, he descended to drink water therefrom. Having drunk water, he had commenced his return, when on a stone he deciphered this inscription; that: "When a King and minister are equal in splendour and power, then wealth forsakes one of the two." Having read this, daubing mud on that stone, he came unto the minister. Then the minister also went unto that well to drink water, and saw it. He said, some one has only now daubed this stone with mud. Again washing that stone, having read the inscription, he said within himself, The King has hidden this from me. Thus considering, having drunk water, the minister came unto the King. The King slept: so the minister killed him.

Therefore, O great King! I say to you, that a minister becoming powerful, regards himself in the light of a King, and if a King entrust the Kingdom to one minister, then he will show pride, and become foolish through pride. Having become foolish, there will remain no thought of right and wrong. It is said, "Food mixed with poison, alms once bestowed, and a wicked minister; these never keep near you." O Sire! What is right for a servant to do, that have I related to you, now whatever be your wish, that do. In the world, such people are few, who covet not kingdom and wealth. Therefore I now tell you plainly, he (Sunjewuk) wishes to take away your kingdom. Now know this. The tiger said, Sunjewuk is my great friend, he will never meditate any evil; because he who is a friend, will not become unfriendly. It is said, "Fire burns a house, yet nevertheless, without fire one cannot get on." Again Dumnuk said, O Sire! however much any one may do, yet the wicked and the fool forsake not their natural disposition, as a dog's tail rubbed with oil, though it be warmed by the fire, yet it will remain crooked as before; so if you show respect unto the low, they will not acknowledge the favor, and if you water the Neem(1) with honey yet its fruit will not be sweet. It is said, "He is a friend, who dispels misfortune; that is a good action, from which dishonor is not the result; that wife and that domestic good, who are obedient; he is wise who shows no pride; judicious (prudent) he who retaineth not covetousness; he is a man who subdueth his passions, and, O Sire! he is a good minister who is a well-wisher." Sunjewuk is not a bestower of comfort to you: he is the root of distress, quickly destroy him. It is said, "A King who is blinded by wealth and desire, who discerns not what is for his good or evil, who is besotted by his own passions; and who when through pride suffers affliction, then he casts the blame on the minister." Hearing these words, the tiger thought in his own mind, it is not right to punish any one without understanding the facts of his case. Again Dumnuk said: O Lord of the earth! Sunjewuk to-day even is engaged in an attempt to kill you; you send for him but conceal the secret from him. It is said, "Counsel and a seed keep concealed: if you do not keep them concealed, then they will not bring forth fruit; and of the wicked this is the nature, that first by speaking sweet soft words they take possession of one's wealth and heart, afterwards being inimical they despoil one." As Shukun having taught Durisdhun stratagem, caused him to fight a great battle(2). Pingul said, What can he do to me? Again Dumnuk said, O great King! Do not think this that "I am powerful." It is said, "Finding an opportunity, the small do great things," just as a partridge distressed the ocean much. The King inquired, What is that story? Then Dumnuk began to relate :—

On the sea-shore a male and female partridge dwelt. When the female became pregnant, then said she to her husband, O Lord! Show me a place

(1) Neem is the *Melia Azedirachta*, or Margosa tree, whose leaves steeped in hot water are often used for the cure of wounds among natives, or else ground fine and put on. They are taken by some medicinally.

(2) Called महाभारत, or the great war between the Kurus and Pandus, the descendants of Bharat.

to deposit my eggs in. He replied: This is a good place. Then the female said: Here the lofty waves of the sea coming, will give me trouble. The partridge replied: If the sea give me trouble, I will then remedy it. Again the female said, smiling: What are you compared with the ocean? (lit: where are you, where the ocean?) Therefore first reflect, then act so that afterwards there will be no distress. Then the partridge said, Lay your eggs with unconcern, then the rest I will settle. Hearing these words, she there gave eggs. And the sea, for the sake of trying the partridge's power, took and washed away the eggs with its waves. Then the female said, O Lord! the eggs has the sea taken and washed away: do what you can now. The partridge said, O beloved! do not have a care. I will now come back with them. Saying thus much, having taken all the birds with him, he went unto the Adjutant(1) and the Adjutant went and told Shri Narain. Shri Narain punished the sea, and gave it orders. It gave up the eggs afterwards, then the partridge with all the birds, taking the eggs, returned home. Therefore, O great King! I say that, "Until called into play no one's strength can be ascertained." Again said the King: How can I discover that he (Sunjewuk) is coming to fight with me. Dumnuk replied, O great King! his strength lays in his horns. When he shall present his horns at you, then will you know, and whatever lays in your power that do.

Having said these words, rising from thence, Dumnuk went unto the bullock Sunjewuk, and with a sad countenance stood before him. Then he enquired of his welfare. Dumnuk replied, Friend! How can it be well with a servant? Because his mind remains absorbed with care night and day, and especially the King's servant remains ever and anon terrified. It is said, "Who having acquired wealth shows not arrogance? In the world having come, who has not suffered misfortunes? Whose heart has not become in the power of woman? Who falls not into the hands of death? The King, whose friend has he become? A bawd, whose wife has she become? Who has not fallen into the snare of the wicked?" When Dumnuk had spoken such sorrowful words, then Sunjewuk said, Friend, what such misfortune has befallen you that you speak such sad words? Tell me. Then Dumnuk replied, Friend, I am very unfortunate, just as one drowning in the sea finds a serpent, and can neither grasp nor leave it, so even am I: one word there is which I can-

(1) Is the *Ardea argala*, or gigantic crane, the bird and vehicle of Vishnu, and designated King of birds.

not speak, nor can I remain without saying it: because if I tell it the King will be angry, and if I do not tell it then my sense of duty will be forfeited. Therefore am I fallen into a sea of perplexity. Sunjewuk said, Friend, whatever is in your mind, that declare. He said, Brother, I now tell you, keep this matter secret, and whatever comes within your understanding, that do. Because you have come hither through confidence in me; therefore I fear dishonor, and for the sake of our future well-being I put you on your guard, you remain vigilant. The King regards you now with an evil eye. He told me, "I will to-day kill Sunjewuk and satisfy all my family." Hearing these words Sunjewuk experienced excessive affliction. Then said Dumnuk, Friend, do not grieve. Now whatever comes within your wisdom that do. Again Sunjewuk observed, that this is a true saying which some one uttered that "A miser obtains wealth; rain falls on sterile ground; a beautiful woman enjoys herself with low people; the King exalts the unworthy." Having said thus much he reflected in his own mind, Does this one speak this of himself, or has the King thus conceived? Thus reflecting, he began to say within himself, among clean things dirty ones on account of their filthiness receive no splendour, just as from lamp-black the eyes receive lustre, but the lamp-black gains not brilliancy. Therefore to this one, what power could there be that he should speak thus of himself. He (the tiger) must indeed have said so. I truly perform his service with diligence; the King what great offence has he perceived of mine that he has defiled his mind. Again he thought that there is nothing strange in this; for as one performs much service unto a deity, and he for a slight offence of that one, destroys him, so the King indeed for a trifling misdemeanor kills. Now there is no remedy for this. Thus Sunjewuk, having turned the matter well over in his mind, said to Dumnuk, What affair of the King have I so mismanaged, that he has thus thought? Now I will not perform his service; because to serve the King is very difficult. If you act well, he regards it amiss: it is not expedient to serve him; and the friendship of a King remaineth not stable. It is said, "To render aid to the wicked, and to give advice to the fool, is useless." Again as in sandal-wood snakes; in the water green vegetables come of themselves; so in our happiness, distress coming, impairs it. Then said Dumnuk, Friend, a wicked person, at first, on seeing one coming, who respectfully seats him, and with affection speaks friendly words to him, one cannot tell afterwards what mischief he may do.

They say, "For the purpose of crossing the ocean is a ship, for darkness a lamp, for the heat a fan, and the tenter for a furious elephant: thus hath the Creator framed a remedy for all, but the wicked man's mind he has been unable to make any remedy for (converting). Again Sunjewuk said, Brother, I being a feeder on rice-plant and water, subject unto him why should I remain? It is said, "If in the mind of the King distrust (or alienation of friendship) enters, it is not removed. As a crystal vessel when broken cannot be repaired, so the mind of a King once estranged never again inclines." They say, "The King's wrath is like a thunderbolt, but once you may escape from a thunderbolt, whereas from the King's wrath you never escape." Therefore now being humble to suffer stripes will not be right: but rather to die fighting is better; because in heroism there are two points. If I survive, I enjoy ease (on earth) and if I die, I attain unto bliss in heaven. Therefore at this time to make war is expedient. Again said Dumnuk, Oh Friend! I tell you, that when erecting his ears and tail, he shall open out his mouth, at that time whatever strength you may have, exert; in it in no way show laxity. It is said, "If being powerful, one exhibit not one's strength, then he reaps dishonor. As the fire, without heat in it, every one takes up, so do all oppress a weak man." Having spoken thus much, Dumnuk said, Brother, now keep this in your mind. When occasion offers, then will you understand it. Thus saying, and taking leave of Sunjewuk, Dumnuk went unto Kurtuk. Then inquired he of him, Friend, what have you accomplished? He replied: I have come, having caused a rupture between the two. Then said Kurtuk, there is no doubt of that. It is said, "A wicked man what can he not do? on account of his forbearance who is not learned? Again, however wise a man may be, yet by society with the wicked he becomes of a surety defiled; because by society with the wicked what cannot be effected is but little; as fire, wherever it remains it consumes." Thus the two conversed.

Then Dumnuk went unto Pingul: joining his hands he stood before him and said, O great King! sit on your guard. The animal is come to fight. Just as the tiger had got himself prepared, that instant the bullock, full of fury, entered the wood. Then when on seeing him the tiger arose and rushed forth; he, also reaching there, butted him with his horns, and the two animals fought with all their might. At length by the hand of the tiger the bullock lay slain. Then began the tiger to lament, saying, Alas! what is this I have done, that through my avarice for the sovereignty and wealth, this poor grain-feeding bullock having slain, I have brought a great sin on my head! In this world sharers in wealth there is an abundance of, but of sin a participator there is none. It is said, "That tiger is King, who throws down the King of elephants." Then said Dumnuk, O great King! Where is this the custom of, that after having slain your enemy, you are afflicted? In the rules of administration it is written that, "If a father, brother, son or friend aspire to the Kingdom (lit: desire to take it away) the King must destroy them. Though he be strictly just, yet should he not be merciful." Again to a religious mendicant forgiveness is an ornament, so is it a crime in a King. Again in Moral Philosophy it is said, "A King over-merciful, a priest over-greedy, a woman distracted with lust, a servant inimical, a companion ill-disposed, a negligent minister, and he who acknowledges not a benefit received, these immediately should be dismissed, as many as there are." Again it is thus said, "As a bawd, so is a King, in some instances avaricious, in others beneficent; sometimes true, at others false; either harsh or mild, envious or merciful, and ever desirous of more wealth and followers." In this manner Dumnuk explained every thing to the King, and again becoming himself minister, began to transact the affairs of the state.

Having related thus much, Vishnu Surma gave the Princes a blessing, saying; O Princes! may Breach of Friendship be among your enemies, and happiness to your friends.

END OF THE SECOND STORY OF THE WHOLE COMPILATION, BY NAME "BREACH OF FRIENDSHIP."

BOOK THE THIRD.

ON WAR.

Vishnu Surma, when he began to relate another story, then the Princes said, O Holy Preceptor! now to hear about War, we have a desire, have the kindness to relate it.

Vishnu Surma said, O Princes! You listen with a calm disposition. I will relate the narrative on War.

A duck and a peacock were equal in power, wisdom, sovereignty and majesty; but a crow through teachery, caused the duck to be slain, and the peacock to be victorious. The Princes said, How did this happen? Then Vishnu Surma began to relate:

In the Camphor Isle, there is a tank, called Pudyumkel. On a certain time, thither all the birds congregating, annointed one duck, by name Hirnaigurbh, their King. He there began to reign. It is said, "Where there is no King, there the subjects remain not at ease: as in the ocean without a steersman, a vessel cannot sail, so in the world also, a King without virtue cannot live." A King desires a continual increase of subjects, and regards them as his own sons: but the King who supports not his subjects, or exalts them, he will not gain renown in the world. Again at one time, that King duck on a jewelled throne was seated in the midst of his court. There from a certain island a crane, named Dirughnukh (long bill), came, and making his obeisance, with hands joined, stood in the presence of the King duck. Then the King seated him with courtesy, and inquired, saying; Oh Dirughnukh! the country from which you have set forth, tell us the news thereof. He replied, O great King! for this purpose have I come unto you, that in Jumbudwip there is a great mountain, called Bindeachal, there the King of all the birds is a peacock, and he resides on that spot. They perceiving me to be eloquent in speech, inquired of me, whence have you come? and who are you? Then, I answered, I have indeed come from the Camphor Isle, and I am the servant of the great King Hirnaigurbh of that place; for the purpose of seeing your country have I come. Then those birds asked: of yours and our countries and sovereigns which are the better? Then said I, What are you talking about? Oh! the Camphor Isle is like Paradise, and now-a-days the King duck is a second India(1); in this bad country why are you fallen (living)? come and dwell in our country. When I had spoken these words, then those birds were much enraged with me. It is said that, "A snake as by drinking milk increases his venom, so a learned man's counsel entereth not the mind of the fool, but rather on the contrary he oppresses him" As by giving advice to the monkey, the poor birds reaped the fruit of their own acts. The King inquired, How did that happen? Then he began to relate:

On the banks of the Nermuda river is a mountain, at the foot of which stands a Semel tree(2). On it, birds having built their nests, lived with pleasure. Once upon a time, in the rainy season, in the dark days of August, at night time, the lightening came flash after flash, thick clouds gathered round, and the thunder rumbling, and large drops falling, it began

(1) The regent of the visible heavens and inferior divinities.

(2) A Cotton tree.

to rain incessantly, at that time, a monkey, having descended from that mountain, dripping wet, numbed with cold, shivering and trembling, came and sat down under that tree. Seeing him distressed, taking pity on him, the birds said; O Monkey! see now with our beaks, having brought grass, we have raised houses for ourselves: to you indeed the Almighty has given hands and feet, wherefore then have you not made a habitation? If you had erected a dwelling, then now, at this time would you have been living in comfort. Hearing this, that monkey thought: Now, at this time, that these birds are sitting happily in their nests; therefore regarding me learned one in the light of a fool, do they bestow their advice. Thus considering, he smiling said, Oh! when the rain passes away then behold my acts. Saying thus much, being incensed, he sat down silent. In the mean time the morning dawned, and the rain cleared up. When the divine deity sun appeared, then the monkey, climbing up the tree, dashed on the ground all the birds' eggs, and pulling to pieces their nests, said; O foolish birds! He who is learned, what is he incapable of making a dwelling? It is his custom that he does not build a house.

Hearing these his words, the poor birds remained perfectly silent; therefore I say, never admonish a fool. Then said the King, relate what happened afterwards. Again the crane began to relate: O great King! then those birds, being enraged with me, said "Oh your duck, who made him a King? I answered Ho! who conferred royalty on your peacock? On hearing these words, they all rose, intending to kill me, then I showed my prowess. It is said, " Sometimes lenity is the grace of a man, but when the enemy comes to fight, then it is expedient to show prowess. As to a woman, modesty is an ornament, so at the time of sexual enjoyment, wantonness is grace." The King duck said: He who watches not his opportunity, and gets angry, he suffers great distress, and even also if he knoweth not his own strength exerts it, it is like as a donkey, who, not aware of his own power, putting on the skin of a tiger, was slain. The crane said, How happened that? then the King duck relates:—

In Hustinapoor there lived a washerman, by name Bilas, who kept a donkey. On it, after loading burden upon burden, when its back became galled, then that washerman, at night time, arraying him in a tiger's skin, used to return, having left him in a field of corn. The watchman of that field immediately on seeing him fled. In this manner, daily, having eaten in the corn field would he return. Then the watchman contrived a plan for slaying the tiger (donkey), and having covered himself with a brown blanket, going near to the ditch of the field, stringing his bow, he himself lay concealed in a bush. At the second watch during the night, when it was dark, the donkey came, and seeing this one's brown blanket, mistaking it for a female donkey, being blinded by passion, ran up braying; then the watchman perceived, that this indeed is only a donkey, that having on a tiger's skin he has come. Thus saying, being enraged, beating him severely with a long club, he struck him down, and his life departed. Therefore I say, Think well what your strength is, then act.

Having related thus much, again the King inquired, what happened after this, so tell me? The crane began to relate: O great King! those birds said to me, O abominable crane! you having come into our country calumniate our sovereign. Having said thus much, they pecked me with their beaks, and said, Ho! just as the frog of the well, praises the well, so even are you and your King. This good country to leave, and to go unto that bad one, you tell us, O fool. It is said, "With great care rear up large trees, for if you receive not fruit from them, yet you will find a cool shade to sit in. In the society of the low, one's superiority is lost, as if in the hand of a spirit-seller there be a pitcher of milk, yet whoever may see it he will say, in this there is wine. But by using the name of great men one attains preferment, as by naming the moon, a hare found security. Hearing this, I inquired of them, How did that happen? Then out of their number one bird began to relate:

Once upon a time, in the rainy season, no rain having fallen, there became a great scarcity of water. Then a herd of elephants there, addressed their King thus: Your Excellency! here without water we are dying through thirst. Hearing this, their King pointed out to them a pool in the mountain; on its banks a great many hares dwelt. When the elephants went there to drink water, under their feet a great many hares were trodden down. Then a hare named Sileemukh there, thought within himself, that in this manner if the elephants make a practice of coming, then not one of our race will remain here alive. Hearing this, a very old hare, named Bejai said, Ho! Do not fear now. I will provide a remedy for this evil. Having said this much he arose from thence and departed, and on the road as he proceeded onwards, he said in his own mind, "How shall I approach near to these elephants? They would destroy one with a touch."

After this much consideration, he, ascending a mountain, showed himself, and this one, when he had made his salutation to them, (lit: when he had said Ram, Ram,) then from among them, one elephant haughtily exclaimed:

Holloa! Who art thou? This one replied; Ho! I am the ambassador of the moon, and have come unto you. Then said they; Tell us the necessity of thy coming. He replied; His Lunar Majesty having thus spoken unto me has sent me to you, "To-day in that you have come, and drunk water at the pool sacred to Chandra, you have indeed done well; but under your feet my hares have been trodden down, therefore am I much displeased with you. Because on my behalf, the hares are the guardians of this pool, I protect them: for which reason my name people call "Sussee"(1) Hearing this, the King of the elephants said; Brother, in this thou speakest truly. Then said the hare; It is not the custom of ambassadors that they speak an untruth. It is said, "Though any take away an ambassador to slay him, yet will he not speak an untruth."

Hearing this the King of the elephants, being terrified, said: Through ignorance have we come forth, but we will not again come hither. Then said the hare to the King of the elephants: In your mind do not be in the least afraid: your offence, having told unto the Lunar Deity, I will effect your pardon. Thus having consoled him, as it was night, he took the elephant to the side of the pool and showing him the reflection of the moon, causing him to join his hands, he himself exclaimed aloud and said: O Lunar Majesty! these poor elephants, through ignorance have come forth unto your pool, their offence which they have committed, pardon: again it will never happen so. Saying thus much, he dismissed the elephants, and they indeed, having beheld the reflection in the water, thought truly, that the moon had descended into the pool. Therefore I say, by using the name of great people, work becomes accomplished.

Hearing this, O great King, I then answered: Ho! our monarch has great power. Hearing this, those birds laying hold of me, took me away unto their King, the peacock, causing me to make a salutation, and to join my hands, they made me stand in his presence. Those birds said unto their King; Oh Sire! this evil-minded crane, though residing in our city, calumniates us. The King said: Oh who is this, and whence comes he? The birds replied; O great King! this one says, I am the servant of Hernaigurbh, King of the Camphor Isle, and I have come from that country.

Hearing this, the minister of that King, a vulture, said to me; Who is your King's minister? I replied, a tortoise, named Surbugya, he is the prime

(1) ससी means either the moon or a hare.

minister of the whole kingdom. The vulture said, It is said, "He who is born in his realm, of a good family, perfect in the art of war, virtuous, obedient, old, an acknowledged clever man, a discerner of merit, a thrifty man, beneficient and benevolent, him should a King make his minister." Then said a parrot; O lord of the earth! The Camphor Isle lies in the Jumbudwip, and yours is the kingdom thereof. On hearing those words, that King said, You speak truly, it is indeed in our domains. It is said, "A King, a child, a madman, a rich man and a woman, these five insist on obtaining things which are unattainable." Then said I, If supremacy were obtained by words only, then I say my King Hernaigurbh would be King of all Jumbudwip. Again said the parrot; How shall we know this? Then said I, By war can it be ascertained. Again that King said, Go you, and tell your King, that I am coming. Then said I, Send thy own ambassador. The King asked; Whom shall I despatch? I replied, thus it is said, "He who is faithful, skilful, pure, clever, bold, not avaricious, forgiving, patient, sedate, of the same realm, knows the hearts of others, whose answers are not quickly concluded; if there be such an one, he is fit to be an ambassador; send him. The King said, Such as this, I have many here, but it is said, "Send a Brahmin, because a Brahmin is a truth speaker, and void of arrogance." Then said I, Oh Sire! I have heard from the lips of the old that no one forsakes his own nature, as the Kalkut (1) poison found a place on the neck of Mohadeva, but it forsook not its black hue. Again I said, O Sire! send the parrot. Then the King peacock thus addressed the parrot; O parrot! Go you with this crane, and having delivered my message to the King duck, return. The parrot rejoined; The King's commands is on my head (I obey), but I cannot travel in company with this mischievous crane. It is said, "If he remain in the company of a bad man, a good person even will suffer affliction: as by remaining near to Rawun the poor ocean became bridged." Again, as by remaining in company with the crow, the duck and the quail were killed. The King inquired, How did that happen? Then the parrot began to relate:—

O Great King! in the road to the town of Oojein is a large pepul (or holy fig) tree, on which dwelt a crow and a duck. In the hot season, at noon, a traveller, fatigued by the heat, coming under its shade, disarming himself, finding it cool, went to sleep. When after fours hours (or rather

(1) कालकूट The Poison of a Snake, as well as a kind of Poison.

96 min.) had past away, the glare came on his face, then the duck, moved with pity, sat so as to cast a shade over his face, and the crow, on wickedness intent, dunging over his face, flew away. That instant the traveller awoke, and killed the duck with an arrow. Again: once upon a time, all the birds congregating, set out on their way to the adjutant. Among them a quail flew in company with a crow. There on the road a cowherd was taking along a pot of curds, that pot of curds the crow polluting, flew away, and the poor quail was there killed. Therefore I say; O Sire! to keep the society of the wicked, is no way expedient. I then spoke thus; Brother parrot, why dost thou speak such words to me: just as is the King so are you. Having heard this much, he became pleased. It is said, "If having committed an offence against a fool, you flatter him, he becomes pleased; as a cartwright, on being praised, took the bed with his wife and her lover on his head, and danced. Hearing this the King duck inquired. How did that happen? Then the crane began to relate:

In Shrinugur there lived a cartwright, named Mundbudh (or little sense), who knew his wife to be an adulteress, but he had never caught her with her lover. One day, in order to catch her lover, he said to her: To-day I am going to the village, and in three or four days I shall return. Having said thus much, going out, he again came into the house, and remained concealed under the bed. His wife, thinking he had gone to the village, called her lover, and at the time of sport, catching some sound, she thought, that this one, for the purpose of trying me, is concealed under the bed. Thinking this, she became thoughtful, and when her lover said, why do you not enjoy yourself? then she replied; the lord of my house is not at home. Therefore in my opinion this village to-day is empty, and it appears to me like a desert. Then said the lover, if such is your affection for him, leaving you, wherefore did he depart? She replied, O wretch, do you not know this. Listen, it is said, "Whether the husband loves his wife or does not love her, yet it is the duty of a woman, that for one instant her husband she forget not, and that the stripes and abuse from her husband she regard as an ornament. She will then obtain a good name, and be called highly descended and chaste. Whether her husband remain at home or go out, whether he be sinful or virtuous, yet the wife should not forget him; because a wife's ornament is her husband. Without her lord, a very beautiful woman appeareth not to advantage. But thou art a lover, thou art indeed like unto betel-leaf or a flower;

a guest for an hour and met with by chance, accidentally the lines in one's destiny cannot be effaced. Over Brahma none have power. Again, he is my lord, I am his handmaid; as long as he remaineth, so long shall I live, at his death I shall become a Suti (1)." It is said, "She who becomes a Suti gets deliverance; first from all her evil deeds, and again, however sinful and evil her husband may be, yet as many hairs as there are on her body so many years with her husband will she enjoy heaven. And as the snake charmer calls, by the influence of the spell, the snake from the lower regions; so a chaste wife, dragging her husband out from the place of torture, shows unto him eternal felicity." Hearing these words that cartwright began to say within himself: Good is my fortune that I have found such a wife, that she not only saves herself, but delivers me also. He thus thinking, overcome with excessive joy, raised with his head the bed with those two on it, and danced.

Therefore I say, though a crime be committed even in the presence of a fool, he on being praised rejoices. Then the King duck inquired: After this what occurred? The crane then began to relate; O Sire! they dispatched a messenger, he cometh after me. Knowing this, as you deem expedient so act. Hearing these words, the minister of that King, the turtle, said, O Incarnation of Faith! this crane is evil disposed: he having been tutored by some other, hath come here. It is said, "A sick man a physician desires; a learned man seeks for a discerner of merit; a King searches after brave attendants; one invested with power persuadeth his master to war." Then the King, thinking over this, said, "Whatever is expedient to be done that do." The minister replied; O Sire! First send a scout and ascertain their forces and plans: because a King's eye is the ambassador. Whatever King has not an eye in the form of an ambassador, he is blind, and he whose ambassador is a good one, that King, sitting in his palace, surveyeth the wealth of the whole world. It is said, "Pilgrimage, religious orders and temples of idols, are ascertained from the religious writings, and secret words from a spy:" therefore, O Sire! the ambassador who can travel by water or land, him despatch, and at present keep this secret; because if the spell be broken, then the enemy will become wary. Therefore I say, despatch a good ambassador and win the battle. Thus the King and the minister were conversing, when the doorkeeper exclaimed, O Sire! a parrot from Jumbudwip has come, and stands at the royal gate, what are your orders for him? Hearing this, the King looked towards the

(1) Suti, a woman who burns on the funeral pile of her husband.

turtle. Then the turtle said, O Sire! First show him unto apartments, then we will consider. Hearing these words; the doorkeeper departed to give him apartments. Then said the King; Oh! War has indeed broken out. The turtle said, O Great King! It is not the duty of a minister that he cause the King to fight or to run away. It is said, "With judgment if one exert his strength, then with very little labor will his work be accomplished; as by means of a wooden instrument (lever) a man can raise a heavy stone; so can a King with a slight manœuvre obtain a victory." Again they say, "In appearance every one is a hero, but he who seeing the strength of another fears not, keeps his mind firm, him call powerful." Again if, when occasion offers, you perform a work, then will it be accomplished, as in the rainy season the corn-field (produces fruit), and of the great the qualities and disposition are these, that before the time they instil fear (unto their enemies) from a distance, and watching the opportunity, going near them, they exhibit their prowess. In adversity they are enduring, and in the accomplishment of all things are not precipitate. It is said, "Slow water bores a mountain." O Sire! The King Chitrburun (or various colored) is exceeding powerful; to engage face to face with strong foes is not advisable; should any fight he would resemble a moth, with a lamp, or as one destroys an ant with a stone, so would he be slain. Again it is said, "If it be not the time to fight face to face, then like as the tortoise contracts its limbs, so sit quiet. When you find an opening, then as a snake spreads out his hood, so issue forth: because knowing his time, if the small lay plans, then are they able to slay the great. As in the rainy season, the current of a river roots up standing trees; in the same manner, seizing the opportunity, all works come within one's power. Therefore think not of fighting face to face; erect a fortress, till then delay his ambassador. It is said, "On a fort one warrior can fight a thousand." Again the King in whose country there is no fortress his kingdom the enemy can quickly take. Without a fortress a King's sovereignty remaineth not firm. Therefore, O Sire! now erect a fort. It is said, "On the banks of a river build a fort, below it dig a ditch, on all four sides preserve a thick jungle, and a place for ingress and egress, fill it with different kinds of missiles, weapons, shells and balls, and always make a collection of provisions, water, wealth and followers." The King asked; The work of erecting a fort, to whom shall I entrust it? The minister replied: He who is skilful, to him give it. Again said the King; In this work the Sarás truly excels. The prime minister replied: Then employ him. The King then sending for the Sarás, thus addressed him: Look you out a suitable spot and there erect a fortress. He replied: O Sire! this tank for some days past I have kept my eye on, that if a fort be erected in the midst thereof then it will be well; because on the banks of it there is an abundance of grain, and by means of grain all comes to pass. It is said, "Jewels and gold of all things are the best, but man without grain cannot exist; as without salt all is tasteless, so without grain nothing seemeth good." Then said the King to the Sarás: Go you quickly and build a fort. In the mean time a wardour came and said: O Incarnation of faith! from Sungudwip a crow, named Meghburun, has arrived; he is most desirous of having an interview with you, and standeth at the royal gate; what are your commands to me? The King observed; A crow is far sighted, therefore it is expedient to keep him. The minister said, O great King! you have well spoken, but in my (humble) opinion it is not expedient to keep this one, because he is a dweller upon land and is a companion of our enemy. Therefore this one's residence here, is not in any way desirable. It is said, "A King who, forsaking his own ways, follows the customs of others, that King will die in the same manner as did Kookur Dumnuk." The King inquired, What like is that story? Then the minister began to relate :—

Once upon a time, near a town, some dogs came and attacked a jackal. He, being terrified, fled, and going unto the village fell into an indigo vat. When the indigo planter thought him to be dead, dragging him out, cast him into the road; then that jackal, overcome with fear, remained as if dead in the street of the town. There some female water-carriers seeing him lying, inquired one of the other, Sister what animal is this? One said, Sister this is a jackal. Then said one of them, Sister, if we cut off this one's ears and tie them round a child's neck, the witch then will not possess it. A second said, Sister, cutting off this one's tail, if you tie it round a child's neck, then demons and evil spirits will not haunt it. A third instantly cut off and brought his ears. Then said a fourth, break out his teeth and place them on the neck of a child, then no sickness will it ever suffer. Hearing these words, that jackal said within himself: The people of this village are very impious; having cut off my ears and tail now they desire to break off my teeth! for this reason therefore if I fly hence then shall I escape. Thus reflecting, that jackal fled from thence; going unto the woods he began to think: Now my color has become blue, I must therefore act so that I may retain my dignity. Thus thinking, and bringing all the jackals to him he said, To-day the deities of this wood have, with their own hands, cleansed me with medicinal herbs, and anointed me sovereign of this wood. Behold my (holy) color! Hearing this, those jackals, seeing his color, believed his word, and joining their hands, said; Now, whatever be your majesty's command, that will we perform. Then, said he; You all remain near me. So they all began to live with him. When he had thus gained distinction among his own race, then the animals of other forests also, *viz:* the tiger, panther, leopard, &c. all became subservient to him. Then he drove out those jackals, so those jackals, collecting together, having reflected, began to say; Now what shall we do? Then one of them, an old jackal, said, Oh! do not grieve, I have found out this one's secret, that having had his ears and tail cut off, is he come, and hither having come, he has styled himself King Kookur Dumnuk. These tigers and leopards unwittingly do him service. Therefore I have thought of a plan that at even time, when all the jackals are collected, they shall set up a cry before him, then this one, not forsaking his nature (or by his nature prompted) seated among them, will also cry out. It is said, "If the kingdom fall to a dog, yet still will he gnaw an old shoe; his natural disposition will he not throw off." Hearing these words of the old jackal, they acted in accordance therewith. When the King Kookur Dumnuk was seated among the tigers and leopards, he called out; then they killed and eat him.

Therefore I say, O Sire! forsake not your own custom, and the secrets of your house, and the secret meaning of words disclose unto no one. It is said, "The conflagration of thickets consumes trees;" therefore, O Sire! never tell a secret to one of another realm, nor keep him in your house. Then said the King, Oh! so is it: but he has come from a distance, therefore send for him and see. If he be worthy to be kept, then keep him, otherwise dismiss him. The turtle replied, Oh Sire! now your fortress is prepared, send for the ambassador of King Chitrburun and dismiss him. It is said, "A King should not receive the ambassador of another King, alone." Therefore summoning all your courtiers, causing them to be seated, then call in the parrot, and with him also the crow. Hearing this, the King did according thereto. Having sent for those two, and given them seats, he caused them to be seated. Then lowering his head, the parrot thus addressed him: "Ho Hirnargurbh, emperor! to you, the King of Kings, Chitrburun, has sent to say, "If you desire to preserve your life, then place yourself under my protection, otherwise find some other place to reside in." Hearing these words, the King duck, being incensed, said; Ho! is there any one, who will slay this ambassador? Hearing this, that crow said, O great King! give me the word, and I will put to death this base one. The turtle said; O Incarnation of faith! the ambassador is the mouth of a King, therefore he hath committed no fault. Just as he there heard, so, here having come, has he rehearsed it. This one would not speak an untruth, and the speech of an ambassador causeth neither personal injury to you, nor doth it exalt him; therefore to slay this one is in no way proper. It is said; "In whatever assembly there is no aged person, that assembly shines not. He is not aged who knows not what is right and proper; that is not justice where there is not truth; that indeed is not truth from which kindness springeth not." Thus explaining to him, the minister appeased the King's anger. Then the parrot, rising, departed from thence. The minister, then conciliating him again, seated him, and causing robes of honor and ornaments to be bestowed on him, obtained permission from the King, for him to depart.

When he went unto his own King, then the King Chitrburun inquired of him, O parrot! tell us what kind of country is that? The parrot replied, O great King! First prepare the requisites for a war, afterwards I will tell you. The King rejoined, For our fight all the necessaries are collected, you tell us. Then the parrot began to relate, O Sire! the Camphor Isle is like the seventh heaven, and I cannot describe it. Hearing this, the King convened an assembly of all his ministers, and said: Oh! the parrot says, Wage war against the King duck, so I ask of you what is now right and proper to be done? And it is my wish also that I engage in fight. It is said, "Discontented priests, modest harlots, immodest women of high descent, and a contented prince, if there be, then these all, in a few days, truly become ruined." Hearing this the King's minister, the vulture, by name Durdushi, said, Oh Sire! When a King's own ministers, friends, army, and subjects, &c. are all of one mind, and there is dissension among the friends, counsellors and subjects of the enemy, then should he wage war. This is the custom. The King said, In my army behold them all; these are devourers, but of no use whatever, therefore go quickly, call the astrologers, ascertain the lucky moment. The vulture said, O Lord of the universe! Think not precipitately of a march. It is said, "If without ascertaining your adversary, you go into his territory, then the smallest can conquer the greatest." Then said the King; If one desire to capture another's domains, then in what manner can they be taken, this tell me? The minister replied, O Sire! strive, and your mind's desire shall be accomplished, but without exertion nothing will be fulfilled: as by taking medicine a disorder is cured, and not by taking its mere name. Now in obedience to your Majesty's command, I now will relate the rules for capturing another's country, as it is laid down in the Art of Government.

First, then—a King sending for all his ministers, warriors, wealthy men, and chiefs, treating them with courtesy, let him take them with him, and arms, dresses, ornaments, wealth, elephants, horses, let him distribute among his own people, and to each one severally, as is suitable to them, treat them all with courtesy. After this, taking his army with him, let him set out, and where there is a mountain, wood or place of danger, there let the chief commander go forth with collected troops, and take with him strong valiant warriors, and let the seraglio, the principal personage, the treasure, the little folks and the merchants be in the centre. Then let the King and the minister keep a look out over all, and keep in front all the inhabitants of the forest and the dwellers in the mountains. Again if the ground be bad, or if it be the rainy season, then let the King proceed mounted on an elephant. It is said, "In an elephant's body are eight weapons; its four feet, two tusks, its proboscis and forehead." For this reason, if the King retain a great number of elephants, it is well, because an elephant is a moving fortress, and they who, mounted on horses, fight, them the deities even fear; and let him keep the full strength, always, of infantry. Again, on going into another's country, let a King ever remain vigilant, never let him put faith in any one, let him have the sleep of the chief of mendicants; and a King should keep his treasure with him, because wealth is like the life, without wealth there is no influence. Having obtained wealth who will not fight? Man for the sake of wealth serveth. It is said "Man through wealth becomes great, and without it low." Again, the enemy's country having plundered and ravaged, he should lay it waste, because by that the foe will be distracted; and his provisions, water and forage, whatever he finds, he should take and plunder; and his forts, fortresses, tanks, wells, oblong ponds he should break up and destroy; his woods, forests and gardens he should cut down. In this manner should he create different kinds of distress to his foe, and always be pleased with his own people and converse with them, so that his people may think, "Our master is pleased with us." It is said, "As a servant performs his work, and gains regard and kind words from his master, so would he not perform it by receiving a reward and harsh words. Again, when the servant returns, having accomplished his work, then he should bestow a gift on him, and if he do not reward him, then he should increase his allowances, and if he do not even this, then should he pay up the amount of his earnings; and if a master in giving a servant his wages puts him off with to-day or to-morrow, his servant will be sad and in time of adversity resent it." Therefore a King, who desires to conquer his enemy, should keep his slaves and domestics pleased, then, wherever he wishes, there will he gain the victory. Again listen to this, If the enemy's followers remain hungry and dejected, they will of themselves come and join with you, then you will not even have to fight. Again, for defeating the enemy there is one great plan. It is said, "Concert a plan for creating dissension between him and his brother, his sister's son and his brother's son, and show these last attention, and bring his ministers and subjects under your protection, and those of them who fight, them destroy, and those who seek protection, dispel their fear; lay waste the enemy's country, and establish one of your own." In the Shastra or Scriptures it is written; "If a King walk after this manner, then will he win a battle."

Then said the King, I understand the mode by which our conquest and the enemy's defeat can happen, but from the path of Scripture the road of the mind's ambition is separate. In the ambition of one's mind, if one think of the Scriptures, it will not answer, as darkness and light cannot remain together. Having said thus much, the King, sending for the astrologers, and fixing upon a lucky moment, at a propitious time, for the purpose of conquering a country (region), marched forth. Then the King duck's ambassador, coming, said to his own King. Your Excellency! the King Chitrburun having come, has pitched his tents under the mountain Mulayachal(1); protect you your fortress, and discern between your own and the enemy's; his minister is very cunning. I have ascertained from his words, that for the purpose of taking our fort, he dispatched his friend the crow. Again the King duck's minister, the turtle, said, O Sire! keep not this crow. The King replied, If this crow had been dispatched by him, then he would not have risen to slay that parrot,

(1) Mulayachal, or Mulayagir, or Mulagir, is a mountain or mountainous range from which the best sandal wood is brought, answering to the Western Ghats in the Peninsula of India.

and it was after the departure of that parrot, that the King (Chitrburun) called a Council of War. This one came before that. The minister said, O Sire! nevertheless be afraid of the newly arrived. The King said, Oh! If a new arrival renders assistance, then regard him as a friend and a kinsman; being a friend, if he be of no service to you, then regard him in the light of an enemy. As medicinal herbs of the forest, freshly gathered, cure the disorder of a sick man and afford him relief, in the same manner some few new arrivals also, by rendering assistance, obtain renown. Again, as Birbur, servant of King Shuduck, rendered him assistance in a short time. The turtle inquired, O Sire! How did that happen? Then the King relates :—

There was a King named Shuduck, for whom, to sport about in, there was a tank, and in it resided a King duck, named Karphoorkel, whose daughter's name was Karpoormunjuri, of her being enamoured I remained there. Birbur by name, a Rajput, thither, from some country, for the purpose of taking service, having come, stood at the royal gate, and said unto the wardour, grant me an interview with the King. I have come to take service. The wardour went and told this saying unto the King, then the King having sent for him, inquired, what will you take per each day? He replied, four hundred tolas (1) of gold. Then said the King, What others are there with you? He replied, My two arms, and the third is my sabre. The King said, This much I cannot give. Hearing this, Birbur, making his obeisance, departed. Then the minister said to the King, O Sire! for four days, now, giving him the gold, keep him, and ascertain his capabilities, whether he is worth thus much or not. Being guided by the advice of the minister, the King gave him the gold, and kept him. That day, taking the gold, and going unto his house, having offered up half, he gave it to the priests; and the half of that to the poor, hungry and destitute beggars he distributed; and one share, for his own subsistence, he kept. In this manner he, his son, daughter and wife began to live together there. When it was even, then taking sword and shield, he would go, and be ready to attend on the King. One day, on the fourteenth of the dark half of the moon, (or when the moon was in the wane) at midnight, thick clouds having gathered round, rain fell, at that time hearing the sound of some woman crying, the King called out: Is any one here? Birbur replied, O King! what are

(1) A denomination of weight equivalent to half an ounce.

your commands? The King said, See now who crieth. Receiving the King's order, Birbur departed. Then the King thought within himself, this was not right of me, that in this dark night, I should have sent forth the Rajput alone. Therefore following after him, I will just see what he does. In this manner, inwardly cogitating, seizing hold of shield and scimitar, he followed after him. Going on, Birbur discovered a damsel, very young and beautiful, with all her ornaments on, standing and crying bitterly. He inquired of her, Who art thou? She replied, I am Rajluchmee, the fortune of the King. Then said he, Wherefore weepest thou? She replied, For a long time past, under the shadow of this King's arm have I reposed, but now I shall have to leave this King; from this grief I weep. He said, In what manner can'st thou (be induced to) remain? She replied, If you sacrifice your own son, then will I remain, and this King's reign will be unbroken for many a day to come. Then said Birbur, O mother! until I shall have gone and returned from my house you remain here. Thus having said, going home, rousing up his son and wife, Birbur repeated unto them the words spoken by Luchmee. Then the daughter awoke. Having heard these words, all remained silent; after which the son spoke. Glorious is my fortune that this body should be devoted to Dewi(1), and the work of my master be accomplished. In this, Father, occasion no delay, because at some time, surely, this body will be destroyed, therefore, if it come of use to any one, then so much the better. It is said, "If one's science, wealth, life, strength, become of use to another, that one's birth in the world is fruitful." Then Birbur's daughter spoke, If you shall not perform this work, then how will you be freed from your debt to the King. Thus conversing they all went unto the temple of Durga, and with pious adoration and joined hands, Birbur, thus much said, O Mother! may our King live and reign for many a day. Saying this, Birbur, striking off the head of his son, offered it up unto Durga; and began to say within himself, I have indeed discharged my debt unto the King: now being sonless, to live in the world is not expedient. Thus reflecting, and placing his head before the Goddess, he cut off his own head. Beholding these two lying dead, his wife thought, in the world being a widow and sonless to live is not right. This determining, she also offered up her own head. Seeing the three dead, the daughter thought, that being wretched, (lit: without feet) and desti-

(1) Dewi is a name commonly applied to the Goddess Durga.

tute, to live in the world is not good. Thus thinking, having placed her head before the goddess, she cut it off. Viewing this event, the King thought within himself, like me numbers of living beings are born and die, but to be such a brave man is difficult! Therefore having caused the destruction of him and family, it is no longer right for me to reign. Thus, after due deliberation, as the King was preparing to strike off his own head, the Goddess, coming, seized his hand, and said, O King! Display not such temerity, thy realm shall not now be broken. The King said, O Mother! I have no occasion for my realm. Again the Devi said, I am pleased with your piety, and the act of your servant: now whatever boon you shall ask of me, I will grant. The King said, O Mother! If you are satisfied, then grant life to these four. When she had brought the water of immortality from the lower regions, she restored these four to life. Then the King, silently setting forth from thence, returned to his palace, and Birbur also, leaving those three at his (own) house, conveyed himself unto the King. The King inquired of him; When you went thither, what have you returned from seeing? Then joining his hands, he replied, O great King! a woman was crying: by the time I arrived there, she had become silent. I found her not, so I returned unto you. Thus hearing his reply, the King said within himself; This is some most upright man, to what extent can I praise him? It is said: "A merciful, generous, devout, truth-speaking and brave man who boasts not of himself, that man consider an upright man." Then the King, in the morning, being seated in the assembly of learned men, related the adventures of the preceding night, and being pleased, conferred on Birbur the Kingdom of the region of Kurnatuk. Therefore I say, that all new arrivals are not bad. In the world there are three kinds of men: the higher, middle and lower order. Then the ruddy goose said, O great King! this is not a work that ought to be done, but it rests with your Majesty's pleasure. It is said, "Envy of others, the wise and learned never entertain, but if they should, then it would be just as the barber lost his life by envying the warrior, who by his devotion had acquired wealth." The King inquired, What is that story? Then the ruddy goose began to relate:—

In the City of Ayodhya,(1) there lived a soldier, one Churakurun by name, who, undergoing great hardship, for the sake of wealth, paid homage to the saintly Mohadeva: then Shiva, always holding an inter-

(1) Birthplace of Ram, son of Dusrut, who fought with Rawuna in Ceylon or Lunka—*vide* Rammayan.

view with him in his dreams, said to him, Oh! to-day, at the last part of the night season (in the morning), having shaved and performed your ablutions, taking a club in your hand, stand concealed behind the leaf of your own doorway. When any one shall come for alms, then striking him with that club, drag him into your house, and he will become a vessel full of gold; then so long as you shall live, you shall remain comfortable. Having gained this boon, he, the next day, sending for the barber, did according as Bholanath (Lord of Forgetfulness) had said, when that beggar became a golden vessel, then he taking it, laid it in his house. Seeing this event, that barber thought; If to acquire wealth, this is the mode, then why should I not even do likewise? Thus reflecting, having returned unto his own house, he also killed a devotee: then the servants of the King, seizing him, took him away, and slew him in revenge for the devotee. Therefore I say; Never envy others. Then said the King; Utter not by-gone words, for the future, whatever is to be done, that do. Under the mountain of Mulayagir, are the tents of King Chitrburun, now what is to be done, tell me? The minister replied; O great King, I have heard that he has come to fight, but do not you have a single care: we will conquer him, because he has not regarded the advice of his counsellor. It is said, "If the enemy be avaricious, foolish, indolent, a coward, a liar, impotent, one who knows not how to keep his wealth, who disregards the advice of others, him you may slay without difficulty." O great King! before he shall have time to inspect our fortress, country, army and roads and passes, send forth an army to destroy him. Thus is it elsewhere written, "That one come from a long distance, fatigued, hungry, thirsty, alarmed, deficient in vigilance, who has passed the night in watchfulness, and whose dwelling is under a mountain, such an enemy quickly attack." Therefore it is expedient, that even now, our general-in-chief should go and fight with his army, then will it be well. Immediately, on hearing these words from the minister, the King, calling the general, gave the order; Go you at this very time and destroy the army of King Chitrburun. He did accordingly. When many of the warriors of Chitrburun were slain, then he began to reflect. Then his minister, the vulture, said; Now why are you absorbed in thought, protect our force. Seeing the King so alarmed, the vulture said; O great King! it is said, by pride wealth disappears; old age taketh away potency; a clever man dispels doubts; by practice learning is obtained; justice increases renown; by humility an object is gained. And if a King be simple, then in the assembly of learned men he derives no splendor. As on the banks of a river, a tree remains fresh and green, so from good society, the mind of the King is delighted."

Having spoken thus much, again the vulture said, O great King! on beholding your army, being proud, you have displayed boldness and have not heeded my saying. Of that impropriety, this is the fruit. It is said, "If a King departs from the advice given him, then to his conduct is blame attachable. Just as by intemperance sickness is generated, and from sickness one dies, so by wealth comes pride, and from pride distress. Again, before the ignorant, holy writings are as a looking-glass in the hands of a blind man." Thus reflecting, I remained silent.

Having heard these words, the King, joining his hands in a supplicating posture, said to the vulture, O Sire! I have committed a fault, pardon it, and now by some means, what force remains, taking it with us, let us follow the road to our own home. Then said the vulture, O great King! it is said, "As anger rises against a King, a spiritual preceptor, a brahmin (priest), a child, the old, a woman, the sick, so it is appeased as quickly." Therefore be not alarmed, be confident. It is said, "Call him a counsellor, who can put right work that has been misconducted, and him a physician, who can remove the Deliquium(1)." For this reason therefore show no concern; by your glory, having destroyed his fortress, I will conduct you together with our force, to our home, with joy. The King said, There remaineth but a small force, how now shall we make conquest of the fort? The vulture replied, O great King! if you desire to win the battle, then make no delay; this very day, let us go and besiege his citadel.

On hearing these words, the crane immediately went unto the duck, and said, O great King! Chutrburun King is about to besiege your fortress with a very small force. Having heard these words from his minister, have I come. Hearing these words, the King duck said to the minister, What now must be done? The ruddy goose replied, O great King! look at your army, see in it, who are good and who bad; those who are good, give them gold, dresses, horses, elephants, and weapons, and the bad, turn out of your fortress and your army. It is said, "That a King who at one time regards even a cowrie as a lac of rupees, and at another time looks upon a lac as a cowrie, then wealth never forsakes that King." Again, "In a solemn sacrifice, in charity, in

(1) *Deliquium*, or Sunnipāt, is explained by Hindu physicians, to be a disease, in which the three humours are corrupted, viz. bile, phlegm, and atrabilis.

marriage, in public distress and in the destruction of an enemy, whatever wealth is expended, that truly is profitable; and a fool who fears to give a little, loses all." The King asked, What affliction is it, that has befallen you? The minister replied, O great King! it is said, "That if Luchmee (Goddess of wealth) be vexed, your acquired wealth will depart. Therefore bestow alms, that Luchmee may remain subservient to virtue." Again, in the Art of Government, it is thus written: "That in the time of war, a King should satisfy his warriors, according to their respective deserts; because those who are excellent, intelligent, noble, steady, brave, courageous, firm, well-bred: five of them can fight against five hundred; but the ignoble, ignorant, mean, irresolute, timid, shameless: five hundred of them would fly before five." O great King! again, whatever King's minister is careless, his Kingdom truly can never stand, and the King who can not discern his own from his adversary, does not confide in his minister, reckons not the comfort or distress of his attendents; that King never remains free from care. But the King who discerns his own from the enemy's, considers the comfort or misery of his attendents; for him his attendants will render every assistance, giving up their wealth, body and life.

Thus were the King and his minister carrying on a conversation, when, at that time, Meghburun, the crow, having come, paid his homage, and said, O great King! for the purpose of making battle, the enemy have come to the castle gate. If I obtain your order, then, sallying forth, I will engage with them, and be freed from my debt of gratitude to you. The minister replied, When once they come out of the wood, a lion and a jackal are alike; for this reason, do not go outside the fort. It is said, "If a King stand in person and view the battle, then the timorous, like a lion, will fight," therefore it is not expedient to go to the castle gate to fight.

On this hand, the King and minister remained thus conversing, and on the other, King Chitrburun the next day said to the vulture, O Sire! the promise that you made fulfil it. The vulture said. Hearken O great King! if the enemy's warriors be few, or the King a fool, and his minister timid, then the fort will be quickly reduced; but here there is not one such case. Therefore lay a plot of dissension among the people there, or, besiege them, or else, stopping their supplies of food and drink, all joining together, let us shew our valor; then shall we obtain the fortress. It is said, "As may be your power, so accordingly exert yourself." Having said this, again the minister whispered in the King's ear, O King! do not have a care, our crow is in their fortress, he will do our work.

Then, at dawn of day, King Chitrburun, taking all his army with him, went close up to the gates of the citadel. Finding that opportunity, setting fire to it, the crow cried out, The fort is taken, is taken! Then the feet of all the living animals there slipped from thence, all rushing, entered the water, but the King duck, owing to his delicateness, could not fly. Then a crow, by name Surbmetr, King Chitrburun's general-in-chief, he came and surrounded him. Then the Saras stood up to oppose him. At that time, then, the duck said, do not fall in battle for my sake. I will remain here. Take you away my son Churamun, and make him King. The Saras replied, O great King! do not speak such words; as long as the Sun and Moon endure, so long reign without intermission. By your glory I will kill and lay prostrate all the enemy in the fortress. It is said, "When is a forgiving, generous, merit-discerning, comfort-bestowing, virtuous master to be found? The King rejoined, When, in what place, is a faithful, sincere, and intelligent servant to be found? Then the Saras said, O great King! forsaking the battle fly indeed if your death be not come, and if death must needs be, then wherefore would ye die casting a stain on your reputation. If from this perishable body, in the world, everlasting renown be obtained, then what can be better than this? Besides this too, you are indeed my master. The King said, this have you well considered? I will even act thus. The Saras said, O great King! do not entertain such a thought, because by a master giving up his life, the subjects become lordless, and this indeed is the faith of a servant, that, as long as he can do it, he contrive to protect his master. By the rise of his master, he rises, and by his fall, he falls.

They were thus continuing their conversation, when the cock came and seized the duck. Then the Saras liberated him from him; placing him on his back, he went and let him in the water, and himself returning, after having killed a good many, he fell dead in battle within the fortress. Then King Chitrburun coming, took all the treasure in the fort, and cut asunder the fetters and manacles of the prisoners.

Having heard this much of the story, the Princes said unto Vishnu Surma; Oh chief of preceptors! among the servants of the King duck, that one was great, who shielding the King, himself gave up his own life.

Vishnu Surma said, O mighty Princes listen: He did a great work, see, for one thing in the world he gained renown, secondly, heaven. It is said, "The servant who for his master's sake has given his own life on the field of battle, that he will obtain salvation; but he who forsaking his company, fly, will fall into hell, and be calumnized in the world.

END OF THE THIRD STORY OF THE WHOLE COMPILATION, STYLED WAR.

BOOK THE FOURTH.

ON PEACE.

Vishnu Surma said, O mighty Princes! you have indeed heard regarding War; now I am going to relate the story anent Peace.

As when two Kings, having waged war, had destroyed their armies, then the vulture and ruddy goose, in what manner they concluded peace between them, so the whole story of the manœuvre I will relate to you. The Princes said, O Chief of preceptors! we are listening with a good will, now please to proceed on.

Then Vishnu Surma began to relate:—That when the King duck asked the ruddy goose, Do you know whether our people set fire to the castle, or those of the enemy? then the ruddy goose replied, O great King! your crow Meghburun is not visible, therefore it appears that this must have been his work.

Hearing so much, the King meditating, began to say, That I consider this work has been destroyed owing to my ill-luck, in this there is no blame attachable to you. This is the fault of my bad fortune. The minister replied, O great King! in another place it is so written, That when the deity is offended then calamity befals a man, and being in the power of fate, he commits violence, and heeds not the advice of his friends. Just as a tortoise not paying attention to the words of his friends, falling from the pole, suffered pain, so he undergoes hardships. The King asked, what is that story? Then the ruddy goose began to relate:—In the country of Magadh (1) there is a tank named Phullotpul, where resided two geese, Bikkut and Sunkut. Their friend, one Kumbugrio, a tortoise, also dwelt there. One day fishermen came there, and seating themselves, conversed thus with one another; "That to-night let us remain here and catch fish and turtle." Having heard this, the tortoise said to the geese, Friends, did you hear the fishermen's words? Now

(1) *Magadh*, is South Behar.

I will not remain here, I will go to some other tank. The geese replied, remain now for the present, for the future we will contrive. The tortoise said, Friends, you indeed say we will manage for the future, but this has nothing to do with the future. It is said, before calamity befals, if you make your plans, then you obtain comfort, and if you do not, you then endure hardships. As Yadbhabishya, the fish, suffered affliction. The geese said, What is that story? Again the tortoise relates:—

Once upon a time, in former days, a fisherman came to this tank, then there dwelt here three fish. One, Anagat-bidhata; the second, Utpunymute; the third, Yadbhabishya. When the fisherman came, then Anagat-bidhata said, "Now to remain here is not expedient." Having said thus much, he went into another tank. The second said, "When necessity requires it, then will I manage." It is said, "He who finds a remedy for what has sprung up, he is clever; just as a shopkeeper's daughter, in the sight of her Lord, kissing her paramour, made an excuse. The third asked, What is that story. Then Utpunymute relates:—

In Bikrumpoor there was a merchant named Sumudra Dutt. His wife's name was Rutunmunjuree, she remained with her servant. It is said, To a woman, who is great, who is small? her work is in accomplishing her own object. One day then she was kissing her servant's face, when at that time her Lord came and saw her. Then she, rushing to her husband, said: O master, keep not in the house this cursed (lit: thunder-struck) servant, this accursed (lit: struck by the deity) one is a thief. Now has he stolen and eaten coagulated milk, I have smelt his mouth, and the smell of ghee comes from it. Hearing these words, the servant got angry and began to say, "That in that house, of which the mistress smells your mouth, there it is not expedient to remain." Then Sumudra Dutt conciliated them both. Therefore I say, that in the time of adversity, whosoever's understanding is of service, he is wise.

Again, Yadbhabishya said, What is predestined that will happen, why should one give a thought to it?

Then the fishermen having come, cast there net into that tank, and those two were caught. Then Utpanymute remained as if dead. Thinking him dead, the fishermen taking him out of the net, placed him aside. Then catching an opportunity, he went and fell into the water. Yadbhabishya had trust in fate, so he fell into the power of the fishermen. Therefore I say, that if you escape before calamity comes, in the same manner as did Anagat-bidhata, it is well.

Again the geese said, How will you proceed? He replied, Friends, you two hold a pole, by both ends and I will seize it by the middle, then take and fly off with it. Then said the geese, Friend, you have well spoken, but in our opinion, just as foolishness was apparent in the plans of the crane, so even are you acting. The tortoise said, What is this story? Then the geese began to relate:—

In the direction of the north country, on the banks of the river Kaweree, on the Gandhmadun mountain, there was a tree. On it a crane dwelt, under it there was a hollow, in which was a black snake. When that crane gave eggs, then that snake climbing up the tree, would take and eat them. One day, the crane remained meditating, when an old crane asked her, Wherefore are you so thoughtful? She told him the whole secret. Then he said, Oh have recourse to this expedient: bring a great many fish and lay a line of them from the hole of a mongoose to the hollow of the snake, when, having eaten the fish one after another, he shall come, then he will also devour the snake. Having heard this, she acted accordingly, and the mongoose coming devoured the snake; but together with this, climbing up the tree, he also eat her eggs. Therefore I say, form not such plans, as by them may happen your own ruin. If you proceed onwards, hanging by the pole you have seized, and any one say aught to you, that instant, getting angry, you give an answer, and the pole slip from your month, and you fall down, what can we do? He replied, What! am I mad that I should speak? They said, Brother, you know, having spoken thus much, those two geese went and flew off with him in that manner

Seeing the tortoise hanging by the pole, a cow-herdess said, Oh! see this tortoise, two birds are taking him along. One said, if this one fall then will I fry and eat him. A second said, I will take him home. Hearing this, the tortoise would no longer restrain himself, then, being angry, he said, You eat stones. On saying thus much, slipping from the pole, he fell below, the cow-herdesses killing him, eat him. Therfore I say, he who heeds not the advice of his counsellor, he suffers affliction.

Then a crane came, when the ruddy goose said, O great King! this is that crane whom you first despatched. This one says, that Meghburun set fire to the castle, and he had come, having been sent by the vulture. Then said the King duck, never should reliance be placed on the assistance or friendship of the enemy; if you should place it, then just as the sleeper on the tree, falling down, grieved, so will you repent. Again said the crane, O great King! When Meghburun went hence, then Chitrburun said, how we will bestow the kingdom of the Camphor Isles on Meghburun, and remove afar his hardship. It is said, That if a servant return, having accomplished his master's work, after enduring hardship, that he should there and then reward him. The minister replied, O great King! this is not proper; give him some thing else, and take heed unto my words. It is said, According to the rank of one, so let the gift be proportionate, to shew favor to the low, and to throw ghee into the sand, is equivalent. Again, if you exalt the low, then you will be like the chief of the devotees. The King said, What is that story? Then the vulture began to relate:—

In the sacred grove of Gautama(1) the saint, there resided a devotee, by name Mahatuppee. In his abode, having slipped from the mouth of a crow, a young mouse fell. Seeing him, taking commpassion on him, the devotee kept him by him, and having fed him with rice, he brought him up. Then a cat used to come with a design of devouring him. Seeing this, the devotee, reading an incantation, turned him into a cat. Again a dog began to come, then he made him a dog. Again a tiger used to come, then he changed him into a tiger; but in his own mind regarded him as a mouse. Seeing these events, the people of the village began to say, Oh! see this, from a mouse has become a tiger; this is through the kindness of the devotee. Hearing these words, that tiger reflected in his own mind, that, so long as the devotee shall remain, till then all people will continue speaking thus of me; therefore I will slay and devour this devotee, then this calumny will be got rid of. Thus having resolved in his mind, he went to devour the devotee. Then the devotee knowing his inward thought, changed him into a mouse as he was at first. Therefore I say, O great King! bestow not a high degree on a mean person. This is not an easy thing to do. Listen, as a crane, devouring fish after fish entertained a desire for fresh food to eat, had his own throat cut, so may such never happen (to you). The King said, What is that story? Then the vulture relates:—

In the country of Malao, there is a tank, by name Padamgurbh. Thither dwelt a feeble old crane who always made it appear as if he were industrious. Seeing him from a distance, a crab asked him, Brother, wherefore are your sorrowful; and relinquishing food, why are you sitting so sad?

(1) Gautama is famous in Hindu mythology. Author of the Nyāya, or logic, whose doctrine coresponded with those of Aristotle: the rest of his history is made know in the Ramayan.

He replied, Friend, my livelihood is from fish, so the fisherman says, that to-morrow morning, early, having come, I will kill all the fish of this tank. From this grief then, I have from to-day relinquished food. Hearing this, the fish of that tank said among themselves; at this time the crane appears, as it were, our friend: now indeed our escape seemeth to be through him. It is said, if he render a benefit, then even with an enemy form an union, because of kindness the cause is friendship.

Then the fish said unto the crane, By some means take us in charge. He replied, there is one mode of preserving you. If I take you away into another tank, then you will escape. They said, do so. Then that crane would take one fish away in his mouth, and having devoured it return. In this same way he eat all the fish. Then the crab also said unto the crane, Take me away. This one having a desire to eat new food, carried him off also, and where having been seated he had eaten the fish, thither having taken him he put him down. Seeing the bones of the fish lying there, the crab thought, I indeed see death, but it is thus said, as long as you are terrified there is fear, and when fear seize you then you either die or kill, because if you die fighting, then there remains no grief in your mind. Thus reflecting, he, exercising his strength, cut the crane's throat. The crane died. Therefore I say, never think of performing impossible things. The perfidious never cease their perfidy.

Then Chitrburun said, Oh! it has so entered my mind, that I will give the kingdom of this place to Meghburun, and I will stay at home and receive the precious things thereof. The vulture replied, O great King! by the thought of what is yet unfulfilled, he who looks for comfort suffers distress; just as by breaking the potter's pots the brahmin suffered distress. The King said, What is that story? Then the vulture said :—

In the country of Kotur, one Deoshurma by name, a Brahmin, lived. On the last day of the sign Aries(1) he received from one of his cutomers, an earthern pipkin full of sattu; he, taking it, remained all night in the house of a potter, and placed the pitcher on his platters. Then began he to think over in his mind, that by selling this sattu, I shall receive ten dumris (2) (or $1\frac{1}{4}$ Pice), with that I will buy some other thing, selling that, some thing else, selling that again, something more. In this manner, when

(1) On that day, i. e. the day of the Sun's entering into Aries, the meal of parched grain, or sattu, is distributed by the jajmans (or customers, persons to whose custom Brahmins and barbers have a legal claim) to their hereditary Brahmin.

(2) Dumri is the $\frac{1}{8}$ of a Paisa.

my wealth shall increase, then buying cocoanut and betel I will carry on an extensive trade. Having increased my wealth, I will make four marriages. It is said, A Brahmin can make four marriages(1) and marry into each of the four tribes. A Khatre (warrior caste) three marriages; Bais (Rajputs or merchants) two marriages; Shudra (one of the menial caste) one marriage. Then when those wives shall fight amongst themselves, I will see whose fault it is, and in order to strike her, I will hurl a club at her. So saying, as he hurled the club, it broke instanter the pitcher of sattu, together with all the potter's pans. Then began he to say, Alas! the aerial castle I had built is destroyed. Again, the potter seeing his pans broken, stripping off his clothes and reproaching him, he turned him out of the house.

Therefore I say, that he who entertains a desire for the future, he will suffer distress. Then laughing, the King asked the vulture, What is now expedient to be done, that tell me? The vulture replied, O great King! If a King misunderstands advice, then his minister is called a fool, just as when an elephant goes into a narrow lane, then the driver is called a simpleton. Therefore I say, then that by your virtue and renown, and by my contrivance, the fortress has come into our possession, and the world also knows of your victory: but now proceed to your own country, then will it be well, otherwise the rains may come over head and the enemy be equal (in force.) For this reason if you delay now, then will it be difficult to get out of a foreign country. Therefore in my opinion, meeting King Hiranyagurbh with pleasure, having formed a re-conciliation, you should set out for your own country. It is said, The minister who follows justice, he speaks to the King both pleasing and disagreeable things, and the King also, with reflection, or without reflection, consents to them; such a minister regard as a benefactor to his King. Again it is said, He who is your equal, with him form friendship; because fighting is like the edge of a scimitar, that looks both ways. Again, to be slain in battle, is the same as if friends, wealth, women, fame and your own life had to be given up into the hands of death. Then said the King, If such was the case, why did you not at first tell me, that I might have remained at home? The minister said, O great King! from the commencement to the end you did not heed my words: my will was not to wage war, because Hiranyagurbh's qualities are worthy of friendship; think not of bearing enmity

(1) Among Hindus there are four tribes or classes.

against him. It is said, He who is true-speaking, powerful, virtuous, renowned and who has won many battles, whose relations and friends are numerous, with him you should not make war; because a truth-speaker fulfils his word; against a powerful man, strength will not avail; the virtuous cannot be won over: in adversity his virtue becomes of assistance to him; from the very name of the renowned, people will fly; he who has won many battles, by his fame all will be terrified; and he who has numerous brethren, he will never be defeated. For this reason I say, O great King! now make peace; for all these qualities are in King Hiranyagurbh.

Having heard these words, the ambassador of the King duck went and related them precisely in the same way to his King. Then the ruddy goose said to the ambassador; Brother! these are indeed joyous words you have spoken. Again having gone, bring news. The ambassador departed. Then the King duck asked the ruddy goose; Why did you evince happiness, tell me that? The minister replied, O great King! it is said, With so many form not peace: A boy, an old man, a sick-man, a covetous man, a coward, a religious ascetick, a contemner of the gods and priests. Because the strength of a child is very diminutive, therefore he can neither give punishment, or show kindness, for which reason no one would give themselves to his company. The old and sick are void of happiness, they can be easily killed. A covetous man will make peace in the end; this know, no one fights against him. A coward of his own accord flies from the battle-field. A religious ascetick is sad with every one, he gives his mind to nothing; consequently he is defeated through himself. A contemner of the gods and priests, through his impiety, is ruined by himself. Therefore such enemies should be waged war against and slain. Again it is said, A King who is learned, understands military tactics, knows the country and the times, distinguishes friend from foe, brings his mind to consider virtue and vice, remains with supremacy, speaks everywhere in a manner suitable, administering justice, speaks the truth, in his judgment never shows partiality to any one, and who keeps his counsel close, that King enjoys the sovereignty of the entire world. Having spoken thus much, the ruddy goose again said, O great King! although the minister vulture advised him to make peace, yet the King Chitrburun is very proud, he did not heed his advice. It is said, Without fear, friendship is not formed, and by making peace there is welfare to both sides. For this reason, one thing has come in my mind, if it happen, then it will be well. That the King of Sinhaldweep, a Saras, is my intimate friend. His name is Mahabul (very powerful). I will write to him, that advancing on the Jambudeep of that Chitrburun, he may tread it down, and here you having collected your army together create affliction in his army. Day and night, in their rising and retiring, egress and ingress, oppress them, then indeed you will obtain a victory. It is said, If both sides should become heated, then would they unite like heated iron. The King said, What you think best, that do. Then the ruddy goose, giving a letter to a crane named Bichitr, dispatched him to Simhaldweep, and there, immediately on receiving the letter, the Saras rushed to the attack.

Then the minister, the vulture, said to King Chitrburun, O great King! this Meghburun crow remained for some days in the fort, ask him if the King duck is worthy of forming friendship with or not. Then the King asked the crow, Oh! what like are the King duck and his minister? The crow replied, O great King! the King duck is a modern Judishtar (1), and on the earth there is not another so intelligent as the minister (Chakurbaca) ruddy goose. The King asked him, How did you deceive him, and thither in what manner did you contrive to remain? The crow replied, O great King, he in whom a King places confidence, what great matter is it for that one to deceive him? Just as if one sleep in another's lap and that other kill him, then what power has the sleeper?

The ruddy goose on seeing me, detected me, but the King duck heeded not his minister's words. By this, then, I deceived him, and was allowed to remain there. O great King! the King duck is very brave and truth-speaking. It is said, If one is himself a truth-speaker, he believes others to be even as himself; just as a truth-speaking Brahmin, believing the words of others to be true, lost his he-goat. The King asked, What is that ancedote? Then the crow began to relate:—In the grove of Gautama, a Brahmin was taking along on his head a goat for sacrifice. Three imposters, seeing him, consulted among themselves how to take the goat away, and those three, assuming the appearance of religious men, went and sat down in three different places. When the Brahmin went near the first holy man, then he said, Oh Brahmin! why do you take along the dog on your head? He replied, It is not a dog, it is a goat for a

(1) Judishtar, son of King Pandu, one of four brothers.

sacrifice. Hearing this, that holy man remained silent. Then he went near the second. Again he also said, Oh deity! why have you put a dog upon your head? Having heard this much, taking offence, he lifted it oft his head, and looked at it, and proceeded on thus doubting. "Whoever sees it, they call it a dog, but in my eyes it appears to be a goat." Thus cogitating, he reached the third: then he also said, Oh Brahmin! cast off the dog from your head; what impropriety is this that you have committed, that you have placed a dog on your head?

On hearing these words from that one's mouth, thinking it to be a dog, the Brahmin dashed it from off his head, and took his own road, and they taking the goat, fulfilled their own hearts' desires. Therefore I say, That on hearing the words of the base, the wisdom of the virtuous even departs. Again, just as a tiger slew and eat the camel Chitrburun. The King inquired; What is that story? The crow then relates it:—

In a certain forest, there was a tiger, named Madotcat. He had three attendants, one a leopard, the second a crow, the third a jackal. Those three, one day, perceived a camel in that forest, then they asked him, Where hast thou come from? He replied, I have hither come, having strayed from my companion. Hearing this, those three conducted him along and introduced him to the tiger. The tiger also having guaranteed him his life, kept him, and gave him the name of Chitrburun. Then he, having become familiar with them all, began to live there.

Some days afterwards, in the rainy season, there were incessant showers, and in that time food could not be collected, then those three said, each to the other; Brother, now let us form some such contrivance, that the tiger may slay the camel, then we shall get food to eat. The leopard said, Friends, the tiger has guaranteed him a safe conduct, how can he slay him? The crow said, Oh! when occasion offers, even a King commits sin: just as a hungry female snake devoured her own eggs—what will not a hungry person do? It is said, "The intoxicated, careless, sick, old, irresolute, lustful, irritable, covetous, hungry, &c. neither comprehend nor heed any impiety." Thus conversing, they went unto the tiger, and with joined hands stood before him. Then inquired he of them; Have you procured aught to eat? They replied, O great King! we have made many exertions but nothing has come into our possession. The tiger said, How shall I now exist? Again the crow said, Your majesty abandons the food that has come into your possession, therefore it is not to be found in any other spot even. The tiger said, Say how? Bending down, he whispered in his ear; Slay and eat this Chitrburun. He said, Him to whom I have given a safe conduct, how shall I slay? It is said, The bestowal of land, gold, grain, &c. is a great gift, but to shelter the refugee, gives more fruit than even these. Then said the crow, O great King! do not you slay him, we will form such a plan, that giving up his life of his own accord, he shall present his own head to you. Hearing this the tiger remained silent. Then the crow, perceiving the wish of his heart, acting with stratagem, said to Chitrburun; The King has indeed guaranteed you a safe conduct, yet, at this time you comfort him with food, then the King will be very much gratified. Having thus cajoled him, and taken him unto the King, those three, with joined hands said, O great King, this Chitrburun says, that food is nowhere to be procured, and you have been for many days an hungered, I cannot witness your distress, therefore slay and eat me. It is said, The protection of the subjects is from the King; the root of the subjects is their ruler, and if the root remains, then branches, leaves, flowers, fruits come of their own accord.

Then said the tiger, If one be burned to death, it is well, but one should never commit such an act. Then the jackal said, O great King! it is even so said. Then Chitrburun, perceiving the resoluteness of the tiger, on this, by way of pleasing him, said, O great King! Let your Majesty eat my body. On hearing these words from his mouth, the tiger rushed at him, and slew him, and all joining together made him their food. O great King! therefore I say, That by the stratagem and advice of the bad the mind even of the virtuous is shaken.

Again the King Chitrburun said, Oh Meghburun! how did you remain so many days in the midst of the enemy, and in what manner was friendship accomplished between you and them? The crow replied, O great King! it is said, You should even place the enemy on your head, (show him respect) in order to perform your master's work, and so let him fall, as a river constantly washing the foot of a tree causes it to fall: again, he who is wise for his own object's sake, showing respect even to the enemy, will accomplish his own work, just as the old snake, mounting the frog on his head, eat him. The King asked, What is that story? Then the crow relates:—

In a certain forest, there lived a very old snake, called Nundbish. He could not go about after food, therefore he remained lying on the side of a tank. One day, a frog saw him from a distance, and said. Oh! in that you search not after food but remain lying here, why is it? He replied; Where shall I go, and who enquireth after an unfortunate one such as me? Hearing this, and regarding him as a learned Pundit, he said, Relate your circumstances. Then the snake began to relate :—

In this Brahmapoora there was a Brahmin, named Kaundinai. He had a son of twenty years of age, a man of experience. I, through my evil destiny, bit him. Then Kaundinai seeing his son, by name Susil, dead, fainting through grief, fell on the ground. Then his kinsmen and the people of the village all came and collected there. It is said, In pleasure, in sorrow, in prosperity, in adversity, in good or evil, those who are his spiritual guide, friend and kinsmen, they will look after a man. Then a Brahmin named Kupuldeo came, and explaining, said to him, Oh Kaundinai! thou art a great fool that thou makest this lamentation now; because this is even the custom of the world that on the one hand one is born, on the other one dies. For this reason what sorrow is there in this? See together with his army such a man as Judishtar exists not, then how could another last. Again, death remains attached to one bearing a body, just as adversity to prosperity, loss to gain, separation to meeting, folly to wisdom. Then again this body moment after moment so dimnishes as in the water an unprepared earthern pot decreases. It is said, The body, youth, beauty, wealth, dominion, friendship, and a residence in one spot, these all are liable to change. Therefore he who is wise, intelligent, learned, he showeth no grief at their departure; and listen, as in the current of a river pieces of wood come and meet from all directions, so is life in this world. The more affection you form for them the greater distress will you experience; because in the world, to remain ever in the society of any in particular cannot be accomplished; and if your own body even you cannot retain, then over another's what power have you? It is said, By forming worldly affection distress so increases, as sickness by indulging in intemperance. Again time so passes away, as the water of a river. For this reason cast off all affection for this world and form the society of the good. The society of the good gives far more comfort than all other pleasures:

COUPLET.

Pilgrimage, fasting, religious sacrifice, the deity, a ruby, spells, a tree, a field,
Each in their time give their fruit, but the good are ever beneficial.

And, friend, listen, just as in the rainy season, leather fastenings become slack, so do the joints of this body in old age. Having spoken thus much, again Kupeldeo said to Kaundinai; Brother, now do not grieve; endeavour to preserve your own life.

Having heard this, Kaundinai rising, said, Kinsman now I will not remain in this well-like house, I will go to the desert.

Then Kupeldeo said, Brother, a social being going into a jungle is blame-worthy, but salvation attends the hermit even in a house. It is said, If a man laying aside all hope of a reward, worship Vishnu, to him the desert and house are alike; and whoever he may be, who remaining in his abode, suffering distress, performs religious duties, alms, worship, fasting and sacrifice, and shows kindness to every living thing, him regard as a devotee. Again, he who merely takes food to preserve life, indulges sexual enjoyment for the sake of offspring, and who speaks the truth, he will cross over the ocean of distress. It is said, Whoever performing his ablutions at the conflux of a river which is the body whose pilgrimage is virtue, its waters truth, its perpendicular banks modesty, its waves mercy, makes his inward feelings pure; he escapes from the pain of birth and death. This world has no essence. Man looks upon trouble as comfort: as the carrier of a burthen on getting a load experiences happiness, so is the condition of man. Then Kaundmai said, Brother, you speak truly, it is even so. Having said this, drawing a long sigh, he gave me this curse: "Be thou a conveyance for frogs;" and, abandoning his household affairs, he himself took up the customs of a hermit. Therefore now I have come to bear the curse given by him.

Hearing these words, the frog went to tell his King. Then the frog, by name Julkund, King of frogs, came forth. Then the snake, making his obeisance to him, mounted him on his head, and took him all round the tank. The next day when he came and mounted then that one could not go. Then said the frog, Go quickly. The snake said, Master, through hunger I am unable to proceed. He said, By my orders eat thou the frogs of my army. Then the snake, joining his hands, said, O great King! you have rendered me great assistance. Having said this he began them to eat (regularly). In a few days, having devoured frog after frog, he also eat up Julkund. Therefore I say, That he who is wise, for the sake of completing his own object places even an enemy on his head. O great King! In this manner even is it that increasing the King Hiranyagurbh's confidence in myself, I remained in the fort. After this King Chitrburun said to the vulture, O sire! now if the King duck will become one of us then establish him, otherwise one of our own people.

The King Chitrburun had scarce spoken these words, when an ambassodor arriving said, O great King! the King of Sinhaldweep, the Saras, has come to attack your country; if you wish to save the city then look to it quickly, otherwise it will be difficult to remain. Hearing this, the King remained silent, and the vulture said in his mind, this must be the work of the ruddy goose. Then the King peacock, being incensed, said, Let this work be, come first let us drive him out. The vulture said, O great King, do not thunder in vain; like the clouds in the winter time, exert and show your strength. This is tact that you do not bear enmity at one time with people of every country. It is said, If many ants even joined together then would they slay an elephant. Therefore in my opinion, O great King! without forming friendship with the King duck, to pass hence will be difficult: because at departing the enemy will pursue us; therefore with thought act. If without reflection you act, you will afterwards repent, just as the Brahmin's wife grieved, having killed a mongoose without thought. The King said, What is that story? Then the vulture relates:—

In the city of Ujjayan, there lived a Brahmin, named Madho. His wife brought forth a son. Then one day that wife, having left the Brahmin to watch the child, she went to bathe herself in the river, and during that time the royal summons came for the Brahmin. Then thought he, If I shall not go, then whatever alms the King shall bestow, that some other will take away. It is said, If in the matter of traffick you do not show dispatch then when the time is past it will not be obtained. Again; If I go, then to whom shall I give the child and go. Thus having reflected, that Brahmin left the child in charge of a mongoose, which he had for many a day cherished, and he himself went thither unto the King. Then a snake came near the child; him the mongoose killed and eat. When the Brahmin's wife returned, then the mongoose, running up, fell at her feet. She seeing his mouth full of blood, thought in her mind that this villain has killed and eaten my son. Thus thinking, the Brahmin's wife killed the mongoose. Then going on she saw her child playing, and a snake lying dead near him. Then grieving, she said, Alas what is this that I, sinful one, have done! that without inqiring I have taken the life of the poor mongoose. Therefore I say, O great King! that without reflection never do anything, and forsake lust, anger, covetousness, affection; because through these defects the Kings Prithoo,(1) Junmaijai,(2)

(1) Prithoo, son of Vena, Raja of Bettoor.

(2) Junmaijai, son and successor of Raja Parikshet.

Rawun(1) and Kumbhkurun(2) were slain. And see, by abandoning their inimical ways, Pursuram (3) and Anwarikh (4) having subdued their passions, reigned for some time. Therefore I say, O great King! if you take my advice, then you will set out, having formed friendship with that King. It is said, First then going into another's territory to pitch your tents is difficult, and having done so, to unpitch them is still more difficult. For this reason there are said to be four plans for the accomplishment of a work:—Policy, gratuity, punishment, and sowing seeds of dissension; but from among them, by the system of policy, a work is quickly accomplished. The King asked, How can friendship be quickly formed? The vulture replied, It will be quickly formed. It is said, A virtuous man, at sight, forms friendship, but the fool understands not anything; or whatever even a Brahmin admonishes him, he neither comprehends nor heeds. And, O great King! the King duck is a very virtuous person, and his minister, Surkay by name, the ruddy goose, is very intelligent. I knew his proceedings from what the crow had told me. It is said, Him who you may not have seen yet, by hearing of his qualities and actions you can know. The King said, What is the necessity of speaking so many words? Now what is expedient to do, that perform.

Hearing these words, the vulture, receiving permission from the King, went into the fort, and sent word of the news of his arrival to the ruddy goose. He, immediately on hearing of it, went and told it unto his King. Then the King duck said to the ruddy goose, Now if in the rear of the vulture more forces should come, then what would you do? The ruddy goose replied, This is no point for alarm, because the vulture is very virtuous, therefore there is no fear. It is said, To raise fears in a place void of danger is the act of an ignorant person. Having said this, the ruddy goose going, brought the vulture to the castle gate, and introduced him to the King duck.

Then the King duck, showing the vulture respect, seated him. The vulture then said, O great King! this fortress is yours, to whom you wish to give it, to him give it. The duck said, It is even so. Again the ruddy goose said, Hearken, ours and yours are one and the same, but now there is no need to say more. The vulture said, O great King! in moral

(1) Rawun, son of Bissusrwa and Naikasi, and sovereign of Lankā (Ceylon), who carried away Sitā, and lost both his life and kingdom to her husband, Ramachundra.

(2) Kumbhkurun, Brother of Rawun by the same mother.

(3) Pursuram, the sixth incarnation of Vishnu, and is the son of Jamadagni.

(4) Anwarikh was King of Adjoodia.

philosophy it is said, By giving money to the covetous, propitiate him; the furious, to him, joining your hands in supplication, sing his praise; admit the words of fools; speak truth to wise men; perform, without hypocrisy, the worship of the gods; show much respect to your friends and kinsmen; make obedient, by gifts and honors, your wife and servant; then, in this difficult world, with happiness will you complete your days. Therefore I say, That whatever is expedient that do. The ruddy goose said, What are the rules of peace, them explain, what is the use of talking much? Then said the duck, How many kinds of peace are there, them enumerate?

The vulture said, O incarnation of faith! I will enumerate them, let your majesty listen attentively. It is said, That when a stronger than he shall come and attack a powerful man, and his strength availeth him not, then he makes overtures for peace. These are the names of Peace—Bhupal, Uphar, Santana, Sangata, Upanyas, Pritikar, Sanyog, Purusharth, Adrisht, Jewun, Atma, Upagraha, Puricrya, Uchichunn, Paribhushan; and these are conditions of peace:—When two Kings of equal power form friendship, that is called a Bhupal peace. They call that a Uphar peace, when by giving presents, amity is induced. When by giving a slave friendship is restored, it is called a Santana peace. When five or seven joining together come between and cause a friendship, it is styled Sangata peace. When Kings by doing one and the same thing preserve each other's friendship, that is Upanyas peace. "Now we will accomplish their work that afterwards they may come of use to us," should any, thus reflecting, agree, that is Pritikar peace. When two princes attack the same enemy and they come to terms on the way, that is Sanyog peace. When two Kings taking with them all their force, coalesce, that is called Purusharth peace. "You slay him and we will remain yours;" when saying thus, they agree, that is Adrisht peace. When by giving land they form friendship, that is Jewun peace. When in order to preserve life they surrender everything, that they call Atma peace. When they send their army for assistance, that is Upagraha peace. When two Kings entertain a feeling inimical to each other, and then, being both besieged by the same enemy, join together, that is Puricrya peace. When, giving up excellent lands, a King joins himself, that is Uchichunn peace. If any shall thus say, "I will give you all the wealth that is produced, but do not come near me," and they agree, that call Paribhushan peace.

Having spoken thus much, the vulture said, O great King! these all are called Peace; but at this time Uphar Peace is good; because, a powerful person, who leaving his own country, comes, having expended money out of his own pocket, he will not depart without taking presents; therefore without giving something peace is not formed. Now give wealth, and make Uphar Peace. The ruddy goose said; Hearken! those who consider thus—This one is of our own tribe, that one of another, they are mean persons, but such is not the consideration of excellent persons; they indeed regard the whole world as their own family. It is said; Those men who look on the wife of another as their mother, and who consider the wealth of another like clay; again who reckon the lives of all living creatures as their own, those in this world are wise and virtuous. Again the vulture said; What is this you are saying? Listen, in my opinion those who coming unto the world have forsaken virtue, for a body which may be destroyed in a moment, they have lost everything. They say, Just as by the wind blowing over the water the reflection of the moon waves about, so also the mind of a living being is always restless. Therefore this is expedient for man, that abandoning all affection for the body he perform that work by which his own (eternal) happiness may be gained, and ever and anon let him keep the society of the virtuous, because it is connected with both his religious duty and his happiness. For this reason I say, If you heed my saying, then do even so. It is said, Truth is equal to a thousand sacrifices of horses, but should you weigh the two, truth, if anything, will be the greater. Therefore I say, Now let both princes, preserving sincerity between each other, form friendship and conclude an Uphar Peace, then it will be most excellent. Because in this the snake will die and the club will not break.(1) The ruddy goose said, You have well spoken. On hearing this, the King duck bestowed on the vulture Durdusshi, jewels, vests, ornaments, wealth, and, taking them, he, being delighted, accompained by the ruddy goose, took leave of the King duck and departed unto his own army. Going there he related all the circumstance of this part, and introduced the ruddy goose to the King Chitrburun with great respect and honor. Then the King also with great honor gave the ruddy goose betel-leaf and presents and dismissed him. On the one hand the ruddy goose came unto the King duck, and on the other the vulture shouted out, O great King! all the wishes of your heart have been fulfilled; now in welfare depart for your own country. Having heard thus much, the peacock set out from thence, and with happiness arrived in his own metro-

(1) Your object will be achieved without lessening your dignity.

polis. Both Kings began to reign with happiness in their respective countries.

Having related thus much, Vishnu Surma said, O mighty Princes! now whatever else you may have a desire to listen to, that tell me. The sons of the King replied, O chief of spiritual guides! through thy favor we comprehend all the parts of the art of government, are made happy, have dispelled our ignorance, lost all the sorrows of our minds, and taken a new birth.

END OF THE FOURTH STORY OF THE WHOLE COMPILATION, BY NAME PEACE.

BOOK THE FIFTH.

LOSS OF POSSESSION.

Vishnu Surma said, Listen O mighty Princes! by reading and listening to this story man crosses over the ocean of difficulty, just as a monkey by his own wisdom was saved; and if one should wish to perform a work through deceit, and should divulge the wish of his heart in the midst of his undertaking, still unaccomplished, he would be deceived, just as the alligator was duped. The King's sons inquired, What is that story? Then Vishnu Surma began to relate:—

On the sea-shore in a certain spot there was a fruitful jamun tree(1). On it a monkey, by name Ruktmukh (red face) dwelt. Once upon a time an alligator, called Bikral, beaten by the waves of the sea, came thither, and went to lie down on the soft sand under the tree.

Then said the monkey to him, Oh! to-day you are my guest, therefore I give you some jamun fruit, partake of it to your heart's content. It is said: "If one, whether he be friend or foe, learned or ignorant, come at meal-time, you should perform the rules of hospitality towards him.

COUPLET.

If an enemy, thief or low caste person come at meal-time,
Those in this world are very generous, who, regarding them as guests, reverence them.

Then that alligator devouring the fruit became satisfied. Then daily he would come and go, speaking and listening to good words, eating fruit and taking away nice ripe fruit for his wife.

(1) *Jamun* is the *Engenia Jambolana*, one of the largest of trees; its leaves are about three inches long and half an inch broad, of an oval shape. The fruit is round and of three kinds, Deeriaie, Bhagaie and Sehraie.

One day she inquired, Oh husband! Where do you bring this fruit of immortality from? He replied, There is a monkey named Rúktmukh, an intimate friend of mine, he, with affection, gives me this fruit of immortality. Then said she, He who daily eats this fruit of immortality, his heart must be like nectar, therefore bring and give to me his heart, I, eating it, will become satisfied, and I will sport with you. The alligator replied, For one thing he is my intimate friend; secondly, the bestower of the fruit; how can I slay him? It is said: "In the world there are two kinds of brothers, one born of the same mother, the other a nominal brother, but look on this (latter) as more than an own brother." Again she said, Listen, to this present you have never been disobedient to my commands, but to-day you heed them not; therefore I suspect that that one whom you call a male monkey, is not one, but a female monkey. So you have become enamoured, through affection for her, the whole day you remain there. This I have found out, for coming unto me, you are in the habit of daily relating all her sayings to me, being pleased, and at night, during the time of sleep, your member remains cold. Now I have discovered that your heart is attached to another female. What more shall I say? Until I shall have eaten the heart of my rival, I will not take either food or water, and, giving up my life, I will die.

Hearing this, being alarmed, the alligator becoming suppliant, said, Beloved! I fall at thy feet; be not vexed. Hearing this, and thinking he had become submissive, with her eyes full of tears, she said: Oh treacherous husband! Up to this day you have fulfilled many of my desires, but now by forming an affection for another you treat me with disrespect; for this reason, by your falling at my feet, my heart burns doubly, and if you have affection for me then why will you not fulfil my desire. Then that one began to say in his own mind, that good men say truly—

COUPLET.

The lines on a stone, the perverseness of youth, the natural anger of a cock,
Like the blue color, will not be removed, though you were to make endless exertions.

Having thus reflected, rising from thence, going unto the monkey, he laid down, being sorrowful. Then the monkey, seeing him sad, said, Oh! what is the matter to-day, that you do not say anything and are reclining pensive? The alligator replied, Friend! to-day your sister-in-law, making use of harsh words, said unto me, "You are ungrateful and do not acknowledge any one's kindness to you, because, such a benefactor, you do not even once bring into your house. Then, being shameless, why do you make a habit of feasting at his house and returning. What more shall I say? If you do not bring my beneficent brother-in-law then will you not find me alive." Friend, for this reason being distressed, have I come from thence hither to fetch you, and thither for your sake having decorated the house with gold and jewels, spread silken carpets, prepared and made ready different kinds of sweetmeats and condiments, and having seated herself at the door, she, poor thing, will be anxiously looking out for us.

The monkey said: Oh Friend! My sister-in-law spoke these words to you in truth; because it is elsewhere said; There are six signs of friendship: to give, to receive, to tell another your own griefs and joys, to hear anothers, to eat at his house, to feed him in your own house. These things are essentially necessary in friendship, but I am an inhabitant of the woods, you are a resident of the water, therefore my going there then cannot be. But have the kindness to bring my sister-in-law here, that, falling at her feet, I may receive her benediction. The alligator replied, Friend, our dwelling is not in the midst of the water. Just as on the sea-shore you dwell on this side, so do we on that side, and if you come not then how can our house be purified? Therefore take and climb on my back, I will take you along with ease.

Again the monkey said; Brother, if it be so then now make no delay, set out quickly. Thus saying he climbed up and seated himself on his back, and he, taking him, entered into the water. Then going into the deep part he begun to proceed swiftly. The monkey then said; Brother, go slowly, the waves of the sea are pushing me off. The alligator hearing this thought within his own mind; "Now this monkey cannot move in the least off my back, therefore why should I not tell him my object, that he knowing his latter end to have come, may worship his own family deity?" Thus having determined in his mind, he said to the monkey; Friend, at the suggestion of my wife I acting treacherously, am taking you away to slay you; worship your family deity and abandon all affection for this world. The monkey said; Brother, what fault have I committed against my sister-in-law that you have taken me with you to kill me? The alligator replied; Oh you daily devour immortal fruit, therefore your heart must be like nectar. Thinking thus, she has a desire to eat it, and in order to fulfil her wish I indeed have borne this sin on my head. It is said, "The fire bearing witness, (1) she whose hand he takes according to the wish of her heart, must he act: this is the duty of man.

(1) The Hindu custom at marriage.

Having heard these words, Ruktmukh, the monkey, perceiving his ignorance, spoke with wisdom and stratagem pleasing words anent his desire, saying; Oh friend: if such was your determination, then why did you not there tell me of it, that I might not have come leaving my heart in the jamun tree, for that was indeed a great present for me to have made my obeisance with, to my sister-in-law. It is said; "It is not expedient to go empty-handed to the gate of the royal residence, the house of the Deity, the door of the spiritual guide;" yet I have then come with you into this very deep water void of my heart. And hearken, every living being has fear, because in the body the abode of fear is the heart; for this reason man moves with consideration. Having put down one foot forward he lifts the other, and we monkies do not put our feet on the earth; therefore Brahma has given us the name of deer of the branch, so, in accordance with the custom of our race, the receptacle of fear, which is the heart, having taken it out, and having placed it in a hollow of a tree, being void of fear we rush from branch to brach, and dance and jump about, and now indeed coming with you, having placed my heart with care in the hollow of the jamun tree, have I come without a heart; being fearless, I have hastened forward with you, although the Almighty, according to the rule of the world, has fashioned my heart, yet it is of no use to me, and you wish for it; therefore what can be better if it come of service to you? It is said:

COUPLET.

Giving wealth retain life; giving up life preserve chastity;
Abandon wealth, relinquish life, forsake chastity, all for the sake of love.

On hearing these words, the alligator, with joy, said, Oh Friend! if matters are so, then give me your heart, that that wicked wife's perverseness may be ended and your life be spared; that the sin of injuring my friend may not be imputed to me. Having said thus much, he turned back. Then they both began each to call to remembrance his own Deity. It is said; Even should a wicked person worship his Deity his desires would be fruitless. The monkey then by his good luck reaching the shore, having alighted from the alligator's back, taking long steps one after the other, went and perched himself in the jamun tree and began to say in his own mind, "To-day have I obtained a new birth, in that I have returned, having escaped out of the hands of this wicked one." It is said; "Him in whom you have no faith in your mind, never place confidence in. You should consider who is worthy or unworthy. Act with every one according to his habits and disposition and do not go on (be deceived by) the sweet words of the wicked, because he speaks for his own advantage."

He thus remained thinking. In the midst of it the alligator said; Brother, why remain you perched up there? Give me that heart, I will go and deliver it to your sister-in-law. The monkey replied: Fatigue has arisen from going into very deep water, therefore I cannot speak. The alligator said; Friend, for man it is thus written, "That overcoming fatigue he should exert himself to accomplish the wish of another."

Hearing this, the monkey, being vexed, said; Oh treacherous fool! curse be to you and your understanding; because has any one two hearts? Now go from hence, never return. It is said; From whom you have once saved your life in him never confide, and if you should again put trust in him, then at length, suffering many hardships, you will die undoubtedly. Hearing these words from the monkey, the alligator being thougtful began to say; What have I, unfortunate one, done? That my undertaking, being unaccomplished, I told forth my stratagem. Now in some manner having created a feeling of confidence in him, I must bring this one in my snare, then will it be well. Having thus resolved in his mind, he smiling said; O Friend, thy sister-in-law had no need of this, but I merely by way of jest brought thy affection to trial; do not admit anything into thy mind and come my way. The monkey said; Oh wicked aquatic! go thou from hence, I am not a coming. Thus also said Gungdutt; "Tell Priai Durson that Gungdutt is not coming again into the well." The alligator asked what is that story? Then the monkey began to relate:—

In a certain well a frog, by name Gungdutt, prince of frogs, dwelt. He became at enmity with his own race; then seating himself on the cord of the water-wheel, coming out of the well, he began to think, "By what device, having slain my enemies, shall I reign free from the evil." He was thus considering, when he observed a black snake enter his hole, and he appeared to him to be well-disposed. Then said he; Forming friendship with this one, I will make a destruction of my enemies. It is said; "One should form frienship with a very powerful enemy in order to slay an adversary, and assume the strength of a lion to kill a hare. Never show a little strength, otherwise you will be assuredly defeated." Having thus resolved in his mind, going to the mouth of the snake's hole he called out, Oh Priai Durson! my compliments to you; come forth. Hearing this, that snake thought in his own mind that he who calls me is none of my race, because it is not the sound of a snake, and I have no intimacy with any one; therefore seated within let me first think over it, then I will slip out. It is said, "He whose natural disposition you are not acquainted with, do not quickly mix with him." This is the word of Jupiter. And if I immediately, without consideration, move out of my hole, then I know not but that an enemy or charmer may seize me; therefore it is expedient I should know who this is. Having thus reflected, he said from within, Ho! who art thou who callest me? He replied, I am a frog, by name Gungdutt, King of frogs, from you may come my assistance, for this reason I have come to form friendship. The snake said, Oh! this union is heterogenous, what friendship can there be between the grass and the fire, but now thou hast come to my dwelling therefore what can I say? It is said, "From whom you look for your death near him even in your dreams you should not go;" but what hast thou thought? Gungdutt replied, Oh! this is true, and I and you are enemies from our birth, but being oppressed by an enemy and disrespected I have come unto you. It is said, "If a thorn pierce your foot you must extract it with a needle, and when you behold your ruin from one enemy then seeking protection from some other powerful enemy secure life and property." Then said the snake, With whom art thou at enmity? He replied, With my own family. He asked, Where is thy dwelling—in a well, tank or oblong pond? He replied, I dwell in a well, built of stone. The snake said, Then it cannot be managed, because it is not possible for me to go there. It is said, "Though food be very delicious eat only a belly full, but do not covet much, for if you show greediness there cometh injury, and you suffer distress." Then Gungdutt said, Oh! It is said thus: "That if you meet with a scout then do difficult places become easy, as the scout of the house(1) lost Lunka (Ceylon). Now I am going to tell you all the secrets of that place. Listen, giving your attention to me.

Over that well works a wheel; attaching yourself to it, descending thereby, having seated yourself in a recess, devour my enemies fearlessly, and resting with ease, be merry. I take you with me, regarding you somewhat in the light of a spiritual preceptor in this my dilemma, for

(1) Bhibheekun was the scout of his own house, for having quarrelled with Rawun, Sovereign of Lunka, who was his brother by a different mother, or a half brother, on the matter of the rape of Sita, and having been twice kicked by him, he went and rendered assistance to Ramachandra by letting him into the secrets of Rawun.

this reason fear not in any way, but going quickly, defend my metropolis. Having heard thus much, the snake thought, By my good luck I have met this spark of his family, and morever food is not procurable by me in this place; for this reason I will go along with this one to that place, then without trouble I will sit and find food. It is said, "When the strength of the body decreases and there is no helper near, then he who is wise thinks of some means of procuring his own food."

Thus having determined in his own mind, the snake said to Gungdutt, From this day you have become my friend, now take me there; whom you shall tell me them I will devour.

In this manner having conversed, the snake came out of his hole. Then both conversing together came to the well; attaching themselves to the string on the wheel, they entered into it and abode in a recess. Then Gungdutt recognizing his enemies, one by one, pointed them out to him. He, selecting them, ate all. When not one of them remained then the snake said to Gungdutt, Friend, how (well) I have performed your work, that slaying your enemies I have made your kingdom free from thorns? Gungdutt replied, Brother, just as a good friend performs a work, so have you done, and given me ease; but now attaching yourself to the string on this wheel set out for your own abode. The snake said, Friend, what is this you say, having caused me to leave my abode you brought me here; thither some other of my race, may be, has come to reside, why will he allow me to enter the hole? From thence you brought me, regarding me as your ownself, now have a thought about my food, otherwise it will not answer with you and me. It is said, "In food and transactions show no bashfulness." Having heard these words, Gungdutt had no answer. Then he grieved in his own mind, That what is this that I, fool, have done, that taking a light I have shown my house; now this one speaks words of strife? It is said, "When you find all about to go then give up half." For this reason I must daily give one among the frogs, my followers, for this one to devour. Thus having determined in his mind, he said, Brother, for your food, from my establishment, take one frog daily, and just as you lived at your own abode so here dwell. That one in that manner then began there to reside.

One day Gungdutt's son, by name Subhdutt, came to be his food. Then Gungdutt ran before his wife crying and sobbing. She said, Oh! slayer of thy family, now why cries't thou? The curse of thy family is on thee, but now find means to preserve thine own life.

Hearing these words, Gungdutt showed much regret for his own act, at length, when only Gungdutt remained, then Priai Durson thought, That between this one and me there exists a verbal promise, therefore I will ask food of him. When he shall say, Now indeed I only remain, then by means of stratagem I will devour this one.

The snake having thus determined in his mind, said to Gungdutt, Oh! Friend, now indeed there remaineth here no frog and I am seized with hunger. Gungdutt said, Oh! Friend, now I and you, two brothers, only remain, but if you order me then I will form another marriage, and establishing subjects, I will fill my house with relations, you give a thought to my kingdom and I will have one to thy food. Now even going, I will call and bring the frogs of the tank; and again, just as before, exactly, I will colonise a town. The snake said, Friend, in this thou hast thought well, by this means thy kingdom will be looked after and my sustenance will also be continued. Hearken, up to this thou hast been my brother, but from to-day thou art like my father.

Having heard thus much, Gungdutt, attaching himself to the string on the wheel, having come out of the well, began to say in his own mind, I have to-day escaped from the jaws of death, it is as though I had received a new birth. Thus having said, he went and lived in a tank, and thither the snake for a long time looked out for him. At length, being perplexed, he said, I, unfortunate one, what have I done that I allowed that one to go alive? I have devoured all the frogs in the well, but until Gungdutt shall not come betwixt my jaws I will not be at all satiated. Having thus said, he addressed thus an iguana who abode in the midst of that well: O beloved! if thou wilt perform a work for my pleasure then I will tell thee one word. Hè said, Tell. This one said, That Gungdutt has gone to a tank to fetch frogs, go and say to him, " Bringing frogs, return quickly, and if they will not come then return thou. By seeing thee that one's hunger will depart." It is said, " Hunger and thirst can be endured, but separation from one's friend cannot be borne." Again tell him, That one said to me, if he think I am hungry, let him entertain no fear, if I should act inimically towards him, then will all my acts that I have done fall into the earthern pan of the washerman. (1)

That one, coming out of the well, having gone to Gungdutt, delivered

(1) That is, all my virtuous deeds will be defiled and lost, in accordance with the idea that the washerman's earthern pan is the receptacle of all impurity.

the snake's message, saying, He said, Let us now, two friends, sit and converse on religious matters, let us have no more thought of eating, the provider of food gives a particle to the worm and a maund (80 lb) to the elephant. Having heard all the words of the iguana, Gungdutt said, Friend, it is said, "What sin will not the hungry commit? the ignoble are un-merciful;" therefore go thou, say to Priai Durson, "That now Gungdutt is not going to come." Having said thus, he dismissed the iguana.

Having related this story, thus much, the monkey said to the alligator, Oh wicked aquatic! go thou from hence, like Gungdutt, I am not again going to thy house. Then said the alligator, Friend, it is not right of you to act thus. Hearken, if you do not remove the defect of me, ingrate, then at your door, fasting, I will die. The monkey said, Oh fool! whatever much thou mayest do, yet like Lumbkurun the ass I will not go again. The alligator asked, What like is that story? Then the monkey relates:—

In a certain forest, there dwelt a tiger, Kuralkesh, and his servant's name was Dhoosur, a jackal. Once upon a time that tiger fought with an elephant. He received a blow on his body, such, that he could not go even one step, therefore no food could be procured by him. Then said the jackal, Master, my life through hunger departeth and such is this thy state that not even one step canst thou go, how can I perform thy service? The tiger replied, Oh! go thou some where, look after an animal, though this is my condition yet even will I slay him. Hearing this the jackal set out from thence. Going near the village, he perceived that on the banks of a tank, an ass, by name Lumbkurun, was grazing; seeing him he said, Oh maternal uncle! my respectful compliments to thee, to-day, after some time, I have obtained a sight of thee, and got rid of all my sin and misery. Having said this, that traitor again said, Oh maternal uncle! this time I behold you very thin, how is it? He replied, O son of my sister! what can I do? this washerman is very unmerciful, he loads great burdens on me and does not give me even a handful of grain, I live by eating only plain grass mixed with dust; just think then from that how can the body become plump? The jackal said, Oh maternal uncle! if you are in such misfortune then come along with me, I will take you to a beautiful place. There, on the banks of a river you can graze on fresh green grass of the color of emerald, and stroll about at your pleasure, and you and I, seated together, will talk agreeable words and dwell there. Lumbkurun said, O son of my sister! this you have well spoken, but you are a dweller in the forest, and I am an inhabitant of the city, your subsistence is on flesh and mine on grass and grain; therefore how can an union take place between you and me, and of what use is that nice place to me? The jackal said, Oh maternal uncle! do not say so, you can remain at that place on the stength of my arm; thither there is no kind of fear or trouble, and many other she asses for the sake of a livelihood remain there; when they came unto me they were very thin, therefore they appeared very ugly, having come to my abode they have obtained ease and eaten much food, therefore having become plump, they resemble in color the Champa, and they, being distracted with lust, constantly come and fearlessly tell me each her wish. From among them, early this morning, one aunt (lit: wife of maternal uncle) coming to me said, That in my dream your uncle became my husband, therefore bringing him, introduce me to him. For this reason set out quickly, otherwise some other one will take her away. Having heard these words, being distracted with lust, Lumbkurun said, Oh sister's son! if such is the case were there fire then even would I go. It is said; There are two qualities in a woman—one nectar and the other poison; junction is the nectar, and separation the poison, again by taking whose name man becomes pleased, by meeting them there will be even greater joy. Then the jackal enticing the ass took him away, and the tiger on seeing the ass rushed at him. Then he, being terrified, fled and came not into his possession, but the blow of the tiger's paw hurt his body. The tiger grieving and lamenting laid down. Then said the jackal; what is this you have done, that you allowed the ass to go? Enough, I have seen your strength, if you could not slay this one then how would you kill an elephant? The tiger replied, For one thing, my body is weak: secondly, I knew not of his coming, for this reason he escaped, otherwise I would pursue and slay an elephant. Then said the jackal, Well what has happened is past; let it go. Now I am going to bring him again, be on your guard. The tiger said, Oh! he who has gone, having seen me, how will he come again any more? The jackal said, You speak of your strength, regarding bringing him I know how. Having heard these words the tiger remained perfectly on his guard, and the jackal setting out from thence, entered the city. Going near to the ass, smilingly he said, Oh maternal uncle! why have you returned hither? He replied, Oh sister's son! thou tookest me away to a good place, verily that I have returned having escaped with great difficulty from the hands of death. What animal was that, the blow of whose paw struck my body like a thunderbolt? The jackal smiling said, Oh maternal uncle! it was my aunt (lit: mother's brother's wife); she seeing thee coming, being distracted with love, got up to embrace thee; but when thou, impotent, fleddest, then she being ashamed laid down there. It is said, "When a woman at the time of enjoyment, becoming wanton, shows her lasciviousness, and by her husband no work whatever can be accomplished, then she herself becomes ashamed at her own wantoness." Now she has said to me, He whose body my hand hath struck, him will I marry; else starving I will die. Thou indeed dost dwell in her heart, verily in her separation from you, she, poor thing, suffers distress: for this reason I say, come quickly, fulfil her desire, who knows but that in the pain of separation her life may not go? then the sin of killing a female will be attached to thee. It is said, By slaying a child, a woman, a cow, a brahmin, one has to suffer the torments of the great hell, and God has made woman the principal thing in this world; for which reason she is dear unto all:

COUPLET.

All call out woman, woman: woman is the mine of man.
In the last moments, before death, behold in the pulse the life of man. (1)

And they, who, entertaining a hope of paradise, abandon woman, to them Cupid gives pain. See some being naked roll about in ashes, some pull their own hair with their own hands, some keeping their hair long seated in the midst of five fires burn, some bending their heads down to their knees and lifting up one of their arms endure pain. Again it is said, "Woman is the root of all comfort."

Having spoken thus much, the jackal again said, Oh maternal uncle! being thy friend I tell thee, because in thy happiness is my own comfort, and from thy distress pain to me. At length the ass, listening to the exhortation of the jackal, being blinded by lust, delighted, then he set out with him. It is said, "That when man becomes in the power of fate, then knowing a thing to be bad, yet he will not mind, and will not remain without doing it." Then as the ass went there the tiger took and slew him. After this, the tiger, placing the ass by the jackal, went himself to bathe in the river; by the time he returned from having bathed, placed his thoughts on his deity, performed his devotions and his libations to his deceased ancestors, the base jackal

(1) The couplet of which this is the translation, contains a play upon the word नारी, signifying both Woman and the Pulse.

through hunger had devoured the ears, eyes and heart of the ass. The tiger coming saw that his heart, eyes and ears were not, then said he to the jackal: Oh! what is this thou hast done, that thou hast taken out and devoured this one's eyes, ears and heart, how can I eat thy leavings? The jackal replied, Master, do not speak so, this (kind of) animal has no ears, eyes or heart, because, had he had ears he would have heard of your name in this forest, and had he had eyes, having seen you, he would never have come again; had he had a heart, having suffered a blow from your paw, he would not have forgotten it again. Hearing these words from the jackal, the tiger dividing the ass ate it. Having related thus much, the monkey said, Oh aquatic! I am not Lumbkurun that I should now come with thee, because thou actedst with treachery from the first towards me, again thou didst reveal to me all thy secret, like the potter Judishtar. The alligator said, What is that story like? Then the monkey relates:—

Once upon a time, in some country, there was a great fall of rain, so that there came a famine. Then the Rajpoots of that part, many of them, went elsewhere for service, along with them, Judishtar by name, a potter, also went, on his forehead was a wound. After some days, going into the midst of some other country, they became the servants of a King. Seeing the wound on the potter's forehead, the King thought in his own mind, That this is some great warrior in that he has received a blow in front. For this reason the King regarded him more than all his companions. One day, that King was seated in court with all his courtiers when he asked this one, Oh gallant man! that wound on your forehead in what battle did you receive it? He replied, Oh sire! my name is Judishtar, for this reason I do not tell you an untruth. I am not a Rajpoot, I am of the caste of potters, and I did not receive this wound in action, I will tell you the secret attached to it, listen. At my father's marriage there were rejoicings, then I also, having drunk bhang (1) in the assembly, was running along in the house, when I tripped and fell. A broken peice of an earthen pan entered my head, of it this is the mark. Hearing these words, the King, being angry, said, He has played a deceit on me, and for his sake, I have shown disrespect to these Rajpoots, now I will thrust and drive him out. The potter said, Oh sire! do not act thus, moreover take a trial of me in battle. The King said, Oh! thou wast not born in a family in which all good qualities are concentrated,

(1) Bhang is an intoxicating drug.

as said the lioness to the jackal's young one. The potter asked, What is that story? Then the King began to relate:—

In a certain forest there dwelt a lion and a lioness, so the lioness gave birth to two young ones. Then her Lord would slay and bring different kinds of animals for her. One day he wandered about all the day but no animals came into his possession. When the sun set, then vexed he began to come homeward, then he found a jackal's young one newly born on the road: putting him carefully in his mouth he brought him alive unto the lioness. Seeing him the lioness said, O Lord! to-day have you found no other animal? The lion replied, Wife, I have wandered about the whole day but nothing has come into my possession. Even now in the road coming along this fell into my hands, so regarding it as a child I did not slay him, I have brought it for your food. The lioness said: Lord, with this my belly would not indeed be filled, in vain wherefore should I slay him? It is said, "A girl, a boy, a Brahmin, these three are inviolable; especially when they come to your house, they should never be slain." The lion said, If thou hast so determined then how will this live? She replied, Feeding this one with my milk I will cause it to live, just as these my two are, thus will this third also remain. Having so said she began to feed him with milk, then when they became bigger, then they, without knowing it, lived together, and the young one of the jackal was called the eldest brother among them. One day an elephant came into that forest, then the young ones of the lion said, Oh! this elephant is the enemy of his race, come, let us pursue and kill him. Hearing this the young one of the jackal, saying thus much, fled: O brothers why go you before this? Together with him the young ones of the lion also fled and these three returned home. It is said, "That at the time of battle if a hero be in front, then seeing him, valor springs up in others also; and if one coward forsaking the fight fly, then along with him all will fly." Then the young ones of the lion coming said to their mother, O mother! this one on seeing an elephant fled, and we also after him. Hearing his own defamation; the young one of the jackal rose up to beat them. Then the lioness said, These are smaller than thee, thou art greater than them, it is not right to be angry with them. He said, These have been defaming me, then what am I? am I inferior to them in family, caste or strength; or, do I not know how to slay an elephant?

Hearing this the lioness, taking compassion on him, having led him aside, said, Son, thou art beautiful and powerful, but thou wast not born in that family which could slay an elephant, Oh! thou art a jackal; taking compassion on thee, having fed thee with my own milk, I have been the means of thy living, so these did not recognize thee, and now between thee and them there has arisen a contention; these will not remain without killing thee; for this reason I say that now go thou dwell among thine own race, otherwise thou wilt not escape alive. Hearing this much he rose from thence, pressing his tail (between his legs) running off he went and joined those of his own race.

Having related this story, the King said to the potter, Listen, thou didst not spring from that race which can endure the heat from iron. Then he removed him from the court. Therefore I say, Oh foolish aquatic! thou hast told thy descent like Judishtar, so what hast thou done? This is politic that where by telling the truth a work is spoiled, and by uttering a falsehood it is accomplished, there falsehood is better than truth. It is said, "If by telling a falsehood any one's life be spared, and your own dignity be preserved, then do so. In two instances there is no harm in telling a falsehood, but if a work can be accomplished without uttering one, then never tell one, and in every undertaking showing restlessness do not speak out without an object." See, the crane by practising silence performs his own work, and being restless, the parrot by talking falls into captivity. Having spoken thus much the monkey again said, Oh fool! for thy wife's pleasure thou didst meditate such an injustice that thou becamest ready to slay me. It is said, If anything can be easily made agreeable to the mind of a woman then do it, but do not be foolish enough in the word of any one to abandon your own faith, because women-kind are themselves self-interested: never place confidence in them, if you do, then just as a Brahmin by putting confidence in one, repented, so would you have to repent.

In a certain village there lived a Brahmin. His wife was very beautiful: her face was like the moon, her color as the champa, deer's eyes, voice like the Indian cuckoo, elephantine gait, leopard-like waist, her hands and feet like the soft lotus, her breasts like oranges, hair like a black cloud, her teeth like a row of diamonds, her lips as the bimbaphul (1), eyebrow as a bow; again her nose like a parrot's, her neck as a dove's; in such a manner had the creator fashioned her that it was as if she had been formed in a mould. All the women of the family were jealous of her

(1) *Brijonia Grandis.*

beauty. When her husband saw this circumstance, then abandoning all love for his own house, being obedient to her, and taking her with him, he went to a foreign country.

Having gone some distance, his wife said, Lord! I am seized with thirst. He replied, Dear one! sit thou here, I will search and bring water. Having said this he went to search for water, and hither, through thirst, her life had departed. He returning and seeing her dead began to weep bitterly. Then was there a voice from Heaven, saying, This one's years have indeed been completed, but if thou hast much affection for her then give thou to her thy years. Having heard thus much, the Brahmin, washing his hands and feet, sipping water, being pure, gave her half his life; she immediately got and sat up; having drunk water both proceeded on, and going near to some village they put up in the enclosure of a gardener. When the Brahmin went into the village to procure supplies, then the Brahmin's wife began walking about in the garden, there she saw that a lame man was seated at a well singing, and the bullocks were driving round the wheel for drawing up water with. Hearing his singing the Brahmin's wife became enamoured; going near him she began to say, Oh! my heart is fixed on thee, fulfil thou my desire. He said, Oh lost to thy house! I am lame; what wilt thou do with me. She replied, Oh unfortunate fool! (lit: stricken by the deity and without feet) what hast thou to do with this, whatever I tell thee do, and if thou wilt not do what I tell thee, then I will lay my murder on thee. Having heard this he fulfilled her wish. Then the Brahmin's wife, being delighted, said, From this day this life has been granted me by thee.

Then the Brahmin came, bringing the provisions, and having cooked the victuals, when wife and husband sat down to eat, then the Brahmin's wife also fed the lame man. Then when they had to depart from thence the Brahmin's wife said to her Lord, O master! at such times as you leave me to go into the town to fetch provisions, during those periods I remain alone, for this reason this lame one, who is the servant of the gardener and sings well, if you take him with us then he will always remain near me. He replied, Beloved one! on the one hand on our journey it is difficult to support one's own body, on the other how shall we take and proceed with this lame one? She said, O Lord! bring and give me a pettarah, place him in it. I will take him along on my head in a splendid manner, never you have a thought on this score. Hearing this, he bought and gave her a pettarah. She having put that one in it, took and placed him on her head.

Then going into a forest, the Brahmin's wife thought in her own mind, That this Brahmin as long as he remains, so long I shall not be able to enjoy myself fearlessly with this lame one. Thus thinking, finding an opportunity, having thrown the Brahmin into a well, taking the pettarah with the lame one on her head, just as she entered the city, the King's attendants seizing her, took her away to the Prince. He having had the pettarah opened, when he saw the lame man, inquired of her, Who is this? She replied, Oh Sire! this is my husband. I through fear of his enemies, take and roam about with him on my head. Now I have brought him under your protection, do as to you seemeth best. The King said, Remain thou in my city, I will allow thee a daily allowance. When thy enemy shall come then inform me.

Having said thus much, the King ordered handsfull of grain to be given to her from every village. She taking the same began to live there in comfort.

Afterwards, by chance, some corn-merchant happened to came into that forest. He dragged the Brahmin out of the well. It is said, "If one's year be not completed, then will one escape from the mouth of the tiger, enemy, fire, water." Then that Brahmin came into that city, where the Brahmin's wife (his wife) was. When the Brahmin's wife beheld her own husband, then she went and said to the King, Oh Sire! my husband's adversary has arrived. Hearing this, the King sent and seized him, and said; Oh Brahmin! wherefore dost thou give trouble to this one, and what dost thou want? Hearing such words from the King's mouth, that Brahmin thought in his own mind, That if this one has cast aside my affection, then it is expedient for me to abandon my love for her, because the heart once separated cannot be again joined, like a crystal vessel. Thus reflecting, the Brahmin said to the King, O Lord of the earth! I want not anything from her, nor will I say aught to her, but she is possessed of half my years, that grant me. The King, deeming the Brahmin's words to be false, remained silent, and the Brahmin's wife, not knowing the former secret, spoke out, Oh incarnation of faith! just as this one says in that manner I will grant him his life. Again the Brahmin said, Having washed her hands and feet, sipped water, and become purified, let her say that thy life that I took, that I return. She spoke accordingly, and as she spoke her life departed from her body. The King, together with the court, beholding it, remained aghast. Then when he asked the secret thereof, then the Brahmin told all the secret. On hearing these words, the King dismissed the Brahmin, and himself took an oath that the words of a woman he would never again believe to be true. Therefore I say, Oh foolish aquatic! never place confidence in the words of a woman. It is said, "If one falls into the power of a woman what will he not do, as King Bhoj and Pande Baruch did. The alligator asked, What is that story? Then the monkey relates:—

At one time during the night the Queen of King Bhoj was displeased with him. Then he tried several means of conciliating her, but she did not in any way heed his words, and said, If, becoming a horse, mounting me on your back, you will carry me round the area whilst I crack a whip over you, then I will do as you bid me. Hearing this, acting accordingly, he accomplished her desire. And the same night the Pande's wife also became angry. Then said the Pande; Wilt thou by any means give up thy obstinacy? She replied, Thou art my culprit, therefore I will shave thy head, then will my anger cease. It is said, "He who is very clever, he, understanding the ways of pleasure, falls into the power of love." Then the Pande shaved his beard, moustache and head, and did as she told him.

At dawn of morn when the King came and sat in the court, then the Pande going gave him his blessing. He seeing him, smiling said, Oh Brahmin! why hast thou become shorn without there being a festival? He through force of his knowledge, thinking over the occurrence of the night, said, O great King! when man neighs after the manner of a horse, then without there being a festival there is shaving. Hearing this, the King remained silent. Therefore I say, Oh wicked aquatic! just as the King and the Pande, so hast thou, being blinded by lust, become under the power of woman.

Those two thus remained talking, when at that time an aquatic coming said unto the alligator, Brother, thy wife through anger is about to die and in thy house another alligator has come and resides. Hearing this, being pained, the alligator said, Alas! what have I, unfortunate one, done, that from the instigation of such a wicked wife I have lost all virtue of my religious acts? Then he said to the monkey, Friend, pardon those my offences, because from this affliction I shall quit this life. The monkey replied, Oh fool! although it was right that misunderstandings should take place in thy house, yet it is fitting that thou shouldest make rejoicing at the death of such a wicked wife; because it is said, "A quarrelsome woman and poison are the root of calamity:" for this reason, if thou desirest comfort for thyself, then it will be well for thee that thou remain separated from her. Let her say and do whatever her heart desires; the tricks of women are of various kinds, to what extent shall I recount them, but understand thou from this that those who are clever and prudent, they will never become subservient to them. The alligator said, Oh! I have committed two blunders, thereby friendship on the one hand is gone, and on the other my wife; just as a woman had neither her gallant nor her husband. The monkey asked, What like is that story? Then the alligator relates:—

A farmer's wife was young and he was a decrepid old man, therefore he could not fulfil her desires. She every day used to look out for other men, and through lust, her mind not being centred in her home, she remained sad. One day she happened to meet a stealer of another's heart and wealth: she said to him, O good featured one! my husband is become old, if thou wilt be my gallant, then taking the wealth of the house I will set out with thee. He replied, Thou hast well considered: good, I will come. She said, Then come thou early in the morning, I will go along with thee. Then when it was morning he came, and taking her along with the treasure, set out from the city. Having gone about two miles, he began to think in his mind, That for one thing this one is beautiful, secondly she has a desire after other men, perhaps just as she has joined herself to me she may go and unite herself to some other, then what shall I do? Thinking this, going to the banks of a river, he said, Beauty! first having crossed the river and placed the treasure and clothes on the other side, I will return: after that, mounting thee on my back I will take thee over; she hearing these words gave him the bundle of clothes and ornaments. He taking them, having crossed over, took his road, and off he went. The adultress grieving, with her head bending down, remained seated on the bank of the river, when a female jackal carrying a lump of flesh came there, and a fish also coming out of the water lay on the sand. Seeing it, the female jackal, putting down the lump of flesh, rushed to seize the fish, here, the flesh, a kite carried off, and on other hand the fish, seeing her, jumped into the water, when the female jackal in despair began to look in the direction of the kite, then the adulteress said, You have lost both, now what are you looking at? She replied, I am indeed clever, but you are doubly so, more than me, in that all you had is gone, and you have neither a gallant nor a husband.

Having spoken thus much the alligator said, Brother, mine is indeed that very condition, but now what plan shall I form? In polity for the purpose of accomplishing an undertaking, there are four plans laid down—"Policy, gratuity, castigation and creating dissension." Now among these whichever it is expedient for me to act on that tell me. The monkey said, Oh, never should one give a fool advice. Again the alligator said, Friend, I am drowning in the ocean of grief, drag me out; thou wilt obtain virtue and renown. It is said, "If the ignorant spoil a work, yet the skilful can put it right again." I am ignorant, thou art wise, therefore in what will be my welfare, of that plan acquaint me. Seeing his humility, the monkey said, Brother, go thou to thine own home and fight with thine own race, because if thou shouldst conquer then wilt thou get thy house, and if thou art killed, Heaven. It is said, "With good persons use the expedient 'Policy,' and pleasing them, fulfil your desire, and by giving money to the very powerful, using the expedient of a 'Gift,' accomplish your own work. Then with the bad, the expedient 'Punishment,' and preserve your own self. Again with an equal, adopting the plan of 'Engendering Dissension' by stratagem and strength, kill and destroy him, just as a jackal did. The alligator asked, What like is that story? Then the monkey relates:—

A certain jackal found a dead elephant in the jungle, but its hide was hard, it could not be torn by him. That instant a tiger came. He, seeing him, got up and ran before him, and, joining his paws, said, My Lord, accept this elephant. He replied, I do not eat that slain by any other, this is my custom; for this reason I give this to thee. Having said thus much he went away. Then came a leopard, seeing him, the jackal thought in his heart, That this is an enemy, I must frighten this one by adopting the plan of 'Engendering Dissension.' Thus having determined in his mind, he, going before him, outwardly as a friend, said, Oh! hither why comest thou? this elephant a tiger having slain is gone to bathe in the Ganges, having left me as watch over it. Immediately the leopard heard these words and saw the prints of his paw he instantly turnd his back. In the mean time a panther came: gazing on him, the jackal thought, If I can get the hide of the elephant torn by this one so well and good. Thus thinking, he said to the panther, Oh sister's son! I have seen thee after several days, if thou art hungry then this elephant which a tiger having killed, he has gone to bathe in the river, until he returns, on it make thy breakfast, and depart. He replied, Oh maternal uncle! if I preserve my own flesh then it is well! how can I devour this elephant slain by a tiger? The jackal said, Oh! I am guard over it and I will remain as a screen to thee, eat thou, when the tiger shall return I will cry out, then fly thou. He heeded his words, and just as having torn the hide he put some flesh into his mouth, the jackal cried out, Oh escape! the tiger is come. On hearing this he got up and ran off. In this manner by adopting the expedient of a "Gift," he accomplished his own work. Then resorting to the expedient "Castigation," he waged war against his own race and allowed no one to devour that elephant. Therefore, I say, That policy, gratuity, punishment and engendering dissension, four plans are laid down; resort to each one where it is most expedient in your opinion. Then the alligator said, I will go to a foreign country. The monkey said, Oh!

One Chitrangad by name, a dog, going into a foreign country, entered the abode of a householder, and having eaten nice good food, when he came out then the dogs of the village surrounding him gave him a good beating. Then suffering distress he took the road to his own town and arrived at his home. Then his family inquired of him saying, Tell us the circumstances attending your going to a foreign country, how you lived there? He said, In a foreign country all else is good except that your own race cannot behold you: if any one ask me, then in my opinion it is not expedient to leave one's home under any circumstances. Oh alligator! therefore I say to thee thy wicked wife is gone, but thou art yet able-bodied; therefore form a new marriage. It is said, "The water of a well, the shade of the large Bengal Fig tree *(Ficus Bengalensis)*, clarified butter, newly churned, a meal of rice-milk, a young wife, sustain life, and if you act according to your age then there is no fault in it." Having heard this advice from the monkey, the alligator departed for his own home, and he made a new marriage, adorned his house, forgot all his afflictions and began to live with comfort.

Having completed thus much of the story, Vishnu Surma gave his blessing to the King's sons, saying, May victory be your's and defeat attend your enemies.

Hearing this, the Princes also, having sent for clothes, ornaments and money, placed the presents before him, and making their obeisance, dismissed their spiritual preceptor, and they themselves began to discharge their Royal Functions in the Path of Justice.

END OF THE FIFTH STORY OF THE WHOLE COMPILATION, BY NAME LOSS OF POSSESSION.

The Date 6th January, the light half of the lunar Month, on Tuesday in the Year 1905.

This translation was completed at Barrackpoor, 23d December, 1850.

J. R. A. S. LOWE.

FINIS.